To Jo
Best Wi
Jan Spencer

SIX VOICES
FROM THE HUB

An Anthology of Poetry and Prose by
Sleaford Hub Writers

Jenny Clairjosra
Doris McCarthy

In aid of St. Andrew's Hospice for Children, Grimsby

March 2009

This book has been designed and created by:
Patrick Ooi, Cream Magazines, St. Ives, Cambridgeshire.
Email: sayhock@yahoo.com

It is published by
Sleaford Hub Writers, Sleaford, Lincolnshire © 2009
Editor: J. Spooner

Printed by
J Kirk, St. Ives, Cambridgeshire.
Email: JKirk@cle.co.uk

ISBN 978-0-9561901-0-9

All contents are the individual creations of the members of Sleaford Hub Writers who meet on the first Tuesday of each month at 7.30 in the Hub.

Any similarity to known persons or places in any of the work is purely coincidental.

Based at:
The Hub National Centre for Craft and Design
Navigation Wharf,
Carre Street,
Sleaford,
Lincs.
NG34 7TW

01529 308710
info@thehubcentre.info

FOREWORD

Sleaford Hub Writers was one of the creative leisure activities set up by the Hub's director, Phil Cosker, three years ago; the sessions were held on the first Tuesday evening of each month. This was a new venture for Sleaford Hub, and at the first meeting over thirty members attended, all keen to exchange views, ideas and share an interest in creative writing.

Gradually numbers dwindled over the months to a dedicated few. In February 2008 the suggestion of compiling an anthology of their work with a view to publication was received with enthusiasm, although also with trepidation as they themselves had to take on the task of compiling, editing, printing and publishing the finished work.

The six members decided that a focus for publication would be to raise money for a Lincolnshire Charity; the St. Andrew's Hospice for Children in Grimsby was chosen as it is the only one of its kind in the County and such a small fraction of its running costs is provided by the government. 'Making Each Day Count' is its mission statement.

Fund raising to cover the costs of production began in May last year; letters were sent to local firms and organisations and the Sleaford Target profiled the project with a photo [enclosed] and article, copies of which were sent with the requests. Despite the economic situation so many responded and so generously that slowly and steadily the aim was achieved. A graphic designer who works for Cream Magazines in St. Ives, Cambridgeshire [and normally designs lifestyle magazines for Estate Agents] agreed to put it on disk as a favour. At the moment of

writing, it is being proof-read ready for the printers.

All proceeds both from the sale of the book and extra donations will go to St Andrew's. Our sponsors and supporters cannot be thanked enough – without their financial help, this project could not have been achieved. Their names are listed at the back of the book and they have certainly helped to 'Make Each Day Count'.

We proudly present our first book 'Six Voices from the Hub' and hope you will enjoy the varied contents. Thank you.

JS

If you would like a poem or piece of prose commissioned for a special occasion, please contact Hub Writers on 01529 308710 or The Hub, Navigation Wharf, Carre Street, Sleaford NG34 7TW with details.

THE SIX

Originally from London, **Jenny Claringbold** moved to Lincolnshire in 2001. She joined the Hub Writers last year and her writing reflects personal thoughts and experiences. As a volunteer and supporter of St Andrew's Hospice for Children she has raised both awareness and funds for the charity. **J.C.**

Ray Jones. I joined Sleaford Hub Writers at its inception about three years ago; since then I have seen my first non-fiction work *Bee-seiged* published. Following on from that, I have written poetry and some short stories from life experiences and have begun my second novel, hopefully to be published in November 2009. **R.J.**

Jan Spooner thankfully settled in Lincolnshire in 1981 after having 5 homes in 3 years courtesy of her RAF husband. Teaching in the County didn't leave much time for her favourite hobby of reading but now retired, an OU degree course completed, she has revived another past-time – writing poetry and short stories. **J.S.**

Geoffrey W. Brown. After spending a lifetime working in agriculture, retiring early due to ill-health, I have found new interests in writing and photography, finding them both stimulating and rewarding. Recently some of my work has been published in the *Best of British* and the *Lincolnshire Poacher.* **G.B.**

Doris McCartney, an 82-year-old cockney, left school during the war, aged 15. She married a Police Officer and had two children. She undertook secretarial work for over fifty years, and was also part-time auxiliary nursing in a London hospital. Her poems have been published in sixteen anthologies. **D.M.**

Bryan Hammond is a married man with two grown children and a four-year-old granddaughter. He has had a love of reading and poetry since childhood. Now retired from the police force, Bryan writes short stories and poetry on a full-time basis. He is currently working on a crime fiction novel. **B.H.**

*Group photo by **John Forman***
*Photos in text by **Geoffrey W. Brown** and others*

CONTENTS

SLOW WAY HOME

We're taking the slow way home
With time to spare, we've time to roam.
Not this time the motorway's fast pace
Where drivers fight for congested space.
Slower roads may bring less aggravation,
As we journey to our destination.
Able to relax, the miles drift by,
Time to think and wonder why
We've never ventured this way before
Taking instead the fastest route to our door,
Unaware of this way's picturesque scenery,
The miles and miles of un-spoiled greenery.
Silver rivers, spring from mountains tall
Through dales and valleys to twist and fall
Racing towards the far-off sea
Their captive waters, there to free.
Villages and hamlets straddle our way,
Quaint country inns tempt us to stay,
Offering guests a gastronomic delight
And accommodation for the night.
Sadly homeward we must proceed
This journey, to retrace, we have agreed,
To sample the local fare
And walk in its un-polluted air.

GB

UN-BELIEVER

Global warming, what does it mean?
Lots more money in the Government machine.
Taxes on petrol, taxes on waste.
Taxes on breathing, taxes on taste.

Ice caps melting, the Ozone Layer.
Let believers say all the prayers.
Nobody's taking my four wheel drive.
My Carbon Footprint means I'm alive.

BH

WHAT A WONDERFUL
COLOUR IS GOLD

A bunch of golden daffodils;
A field of ripening rape.
The sunset's glow in an Autumn sky:
What a glorious colour is gold.

A toddler's bobbing golden curls,
A cherished bridesmaid's dress.
Glistening butter on fresh baked bread:
What a lovely colour is gold.

An old gold satin eiderdown;
A treasured cross and chain.
Two new wedding rings, recently donned:
What a beautiful colour is gold!

DM

GRANDMA'S PLUM PIES

Tom and David Thorpe had the previous evening sat around their grandmother's dining-room table listening while their fathers talked about her plum-pies.

It appeared that when they were about the same age as the cousins they would go off raiding Colonel Shaw's orchard. Growing in his orchard were the juiciest Victoria plums in the district. Having filled their pockets they would high-tail it home where their mother would turn their ill-gotten fruit into the most wonderful pies.

The lads were spending the last week of the summer holidays at their grandmother's before returning to school. It was Monday morning and the two eleven year olds were already bored with the traditional games they had brought with them. Their grandmother didn't possess a computer which meant over half of the games they had brought with them were unplayable.

Away from their grandmother's sight they sat trying to think of something to do.

"I've an idea," David said.

"Go on, then, let's hear it," his cousin answered.

"If it was alright for our dads to go scrumping I cannot see why we shouldn't do the same," David went on.

"We could go through the village and down the lane that leads to Colonel Shaw's to see if the plum trees are still there," his cousin replied.

After making sure their grandmother wasn't looking the two lads sneaked out of her garden and made their way into the village. Halfway down the street they met a gentleman, aged about seventy, marching briskly along.

"I wonder if that was Colonel Shaw?" Tom asked, as the stranger disappeared into the village shop.

"He certainly marched like a soldier so it possible could have been."

"If it was him, it maybe there's no-one left at home to guard the orchard," Tom continued.

Breaking into a run the lads soon reached the lane that ran past the Colonel's house with its large orchard. Upon reaching the hedge that border the orchard they glanced behind them to check if the coast was clear before diving into the long grass growing there. Within a few yards they encountered a fox's trail. By crawling on their hands and knees they were able to creep like the fox under the orchard's wire fence.

Tom, having gone first, raised himself up to spy out the lie of the land. Fifty yards or so ahead he could see that the overgrown vegetation gave way to shorter grass.

Beckoning to David he advanced. Suddenly he froze as a figure in a camouflage suit moved across the trail in front of him. To his relief he disappeared back into bushes. Turning to David he asked if he had seen the man, but David said he hadn't seen anyone. After regaining his composure Tom started moving forward again. A little further on his eyes spotted two more men in camouflage suits huddled in the undergrowth. What he couldn't understand was why they didn't move or speak.

This time David also saw them and whispered into his ear that they should turn back. It seemed David's nerves were beginning to get the better of him and perhaps the plums weren't as sweet as they had been led to believe. Not one to give in, Tom began edging forward again but had only moved a few feet when one of the men moved his hand which held a lighted cigarette. There was something unusual about the man, for although he could smell the cigarette's smoke Tom noticed the man never raised it to his lips.

Onward they crept until they reached the shorter grass from where they could see the laden plum trees. A thorough look-around showed that the coast was clear. Together they broke cover and ran towards them. Just as they were about to start picking the fat plums, there was an explosion behind them and a cloud of smoke began drifting their way.

Terrified, the boys looked for a way out. In the distance they could see the drive that led back to the lane. Without saying a word they began running towards it. As they ran several figures in camouflage suits emerged from out of the trees and bushes. Attempting to avoid them Tom spotted a passageway running down the side of the house. "This way!" he shouted to David, hoping it might lead to an escape route. Down it they ran but as they neared its end a tall gate slid across blocking their way. Turning round they soon discovered another gate had closed behind them blocking their path.

Trapped they stood wondering who would appear. They didn't have to wait long for the opening of a door in the side of the house frightened them even more. "Caught you; I bet I won't be troubled by you two coming here again scrumping my plums," Colonel Shaw bellowed as he emerged. "I think my private army has done a marvellous job in helping me apprehend you. What do you think?" he asked, his voice mellowing a little.

David looked at Tom before answering. "They really frightened us but are they all dumb because no-one has shouted or spoken?"

The Colonel burst out laughing. "Yes, but don't be surprised for they're all robots, moveable scarecrows, ready for next weekend's scarecrow festival in the village. My son and I have used our knowledge of 'electrics' to make them. To activate them we placed sensors around the orchard knowing from past experiences that sooner or later someone would be along after our plums. I think it would be a good idea if you told me your names and where you're staying."

"I'm David and this is my cousin Tom. We're staying with our grandmother, Mrs Thorpe, in the village," Tom said.

"Jean Thorpe's grandsons! I never caught your fathers scrumping in my orchard but I know they used to. I've tasted your grandma's plum pies at the village fetes and know they can't be beat. I'll do a deal with you. If you can persuade your grandmother to bake me a pie or two I'll take the matter no further."

"How are we going to do that without telling her where we've been?" asked Tom.

"I've an idea. If I give you a bag of plums you can tell your grandmother I gave them to you for helping me home with my shopping; the rest is up to the pair of you," he said smiling.

The following weekend was a great success. Life-like scarecrows could be found all over the village but the most popular ones were the Colonel's that moved in and out of his bushes. As he stood in his study watching his troops emerging to surprise visitors he was tucking into his second slice of one of Grandma Thorpe's plum pies.

GB

PROSPECTIVE PARENTS
TAKE HEED

They arrive in this world to their parents' delight;
It could be in daytime, but it's usually at night.
The tension is over, now life can begin
For the dear little mites - will they lose out or win?

Clad only in nappies they lie in their cribs;
Gurgling or crying, they dribble down their bibs.
Feeding, changing or bathing their only routine –
Then dressed up for viewing on a large TV screen.

If cute female toddlers they'll be dolled-up in style,
And everyone must cope with each girlie wile.
The tantrums commence when our boys go to school,
While the language they use makes you feel such a fool.

Young teenagers listen, read and digest
To collect all the info, to bring out their best.
They jump up and down to very loud music
And learn all the tricks to ensure that they click.

Well groomed at eighteen with one favourite beau
The girls wear dresses with necklines too low.
Right up to the minute to get up and go –
Let's hope they'll have learned how and why to say NO!

DM

25 ALPHA

Counting the gloss painted bricks in a prison cell wall is a peculiar thing to do on a late autumn Saturday evening. In fact it's a peculiar thing to do at any time of year.

But then, is it any different to counting the bolts and rivets in our partly open cell door, or even the nine little obscured glass panels that make up the window?

The human mind does all manner of strange things from the comfort of a bed furnished with a wooden mattress and pillow. And even more so when its bored with books, games and magazines.

"Hospital fire, move it, 25 Delta. Let's go."

Their response immediate, engines roar into life, an intermittent blue light bathes the guardroom, sirens blare, they were gone.

We, 25 Alpha, collect our belongings and move as we had done on numerous occasions into the initial response area, (an over inflated name for four simple office chairs in a corridor.)

We, along with many other teams in London, are Royal Air Force firemen drafted in for the duration of the fireman's strike and being breathing apparatus trained, our role is search and rescue.

Our chairs face three prison cells where 25s Bravo, Charlie, Delta and Alpha chill out, resting, waiting for their turn in the initial response area.

I sit down to check my kit while my other three team mates stand to do likewise. Where will we be needed, what will we have to do? Even though there are no books or magazines here, I mentally refuse to count the painted bricks in the– "25 Alpha, one person trapped. Shift your a***s. Two green goddesses in attendance."

We move to and into our vehicles calmly but with a distinct sense of urgency. We know our positions and take them for the sixth time in our already ten hour shift.

Not knowing London, the incidents location did not hold a great deal of meaning for me. Our Army driver's instructions were simple, "Follow the police motorcycle," and follow it he did; he appeared to be stuck like glue but safe glue.

Out of Chelsea barracks and left takes you to the Thames, to the right Sloane Square. Any real knowledge stops there.

We turn right and speed through the streets to the rhythmic flapping of the Landover canvas, the oscillating blue lights reflecting off all adjacent surfaces outside and the rising tide of speculation inside.

After about five minutes travelling: "B*****d! Stupid effing b*****d, can't he see us? We're big enough and bright enough." Presumably we've had a near miss as we lunge forward, a result of our driver's hard and unexpected braking. Our crew commander calls for calm and we resume our journey in silence.

Throughout the journey, radio messages flood our vehicle and we listen intently to hear what incidents other BA teams have been called to and the outcome of their incidents.

We arrive amid a fury of activity. No sooner do we climb out but it materialises that Mum and Dad (or should I say, b***h and b*****d) have left their four children while they go for a drink. 12, 10, 7 and 6, the three eldest are safe but where is the six year old?

We don our BAs and I must confess I misread my air pressure gauge. But that did not matter or so I thought.

When all other safety checks have been carried out, I enter the house with one team member close behind.

My torch beam appears like a lance ahead of me piercing the darkness and the thick acrid smoke. We enter the hallway then quickly climb the stairs. Four steps from the top it turns left, and we reach the landing and quickly drop to our knees.

First on my right is the bathroom. I reach up, turn the handle and gently push open the door. No resistance; I lean in and feel behind nothing. We enter the room and scan the floor with our torches. Nothing here. I close the door. We do the same for each of the three bedrooms. We act quickly but methodically. Nothing under the bed. The kids have bunk beds; nothing in them or their wardrobes. All clear, I signal and point to down stairs. Where the hell is she? I ask myself, conversation being difficult between us and the circumstances making matters worse.

At the foot of the stairs we return to our knees. I crawl to my right and push open the front room door. It moves about a foot and then I feel resistance, something I did and didn't want to feel.

I reach in and touch a shoe, a little leather shoe that only a six year old would wear. My hand shoots back as if I had touched a live wire. I feel behind again–a second shoe, then a long frilly dress. I inch my hand forward and find a soft cuddly toy. My low air pressure warning whistle suddenly activates. I am supposed to leave – regulations. My team mate shakes my boot. I turn to face him; he motions for us to leave, but I can't, have to get her out.

I move into the room, heart pounding, our radios burst into life. "25 Alpha withdraw, the child is safe." But if Becky is safe who is this? Whose mummy is frantically searching, and why did Becky's friend stay?

I must leave now my air is desperately low. I grab and pull her, too afraid to look at her, scared of what I will see. She gives no resistance. I extend my arms to pick her up and then stare into her large unblinking blue eyes. I stroke her long flowing brown hair, and thank God for the health of my two kids.

I stand with the lifeless little body in my arms; no amount of training will ever prepare anyone for this. Emotions running at an all time high I laugh. It's difficult to laugh wearing a breathing apparatus, and then I throw her across the room not caring where she lands or what damage she causes.

I then ask myself as we leave, why, oh why do people make draught excluders so life-like and life-size?

RJ

THE BONSAI TREE

Ancient inscrutable tradition,
sees senescent pine containerised forever.
Cascading over unnaturally placed stones.
Wired
Aesthetically pleasing,
but never will it feel the feet of infants.

RJ

SONGS OF LIFE

"Wednesday morning at five o'clock
as the day begins,
Silently closing her bedroom door,
Leaving a note that she hoped would say more,
She goes down the stairs clutching her handkerchief.
Quietly turning the backdoor key
Stepping outside she is free."

You may recognise these words from the song "She's Leaving Home" written by the Beatles. Both the poetic words and the haunting music bring to life a sad tale of a young girl, who leaves home in search of a new and exciting life, to the horror of her devoted parents. The devastation of their daughter's departure is palpable within the song and may strike a chord with the listener. However revered the Beatles may be for their style of music, like many songwriters before them, they will go down in the history of music as gifted and recognisable composers of the 20th century.

But they don't write music like they use to, it's often said. Many people catch a glimpse of today's artists and are all too quick to dismiss them out of turn, often as much for their appearance as the music they play. Yet, their creative musical art has its roots in the history of life too. Something or someone has influenced them to want to express what they have to say in music and song. It may not appeal to everyone but it should not be dismissed completely out of hand.

To name but two, The Beatles and the Bee Gees have both written memorable scores which have been covered by other popular singers, just as various international operatic artistes continue to successfully interpret the classical music of yesteryear. Comparing today's modern composers against the likes of Stephen Sondheim or Rodgers and Hammerstein may be questionable, but some can definitely be equally respected and appreciated. Indeed the musicals created by Sir Andrew Lloyd Webber and Sir Tim Rice continue to fill theatres the world over.

Music formed an important part of my upbringing, from the songs on the radio of the fifties and sixties, to the hymns during school assembly and those sung in church. Whilst at school in the 60s I was involved with the youth orchestra, and was eligible to a student pass to attend the Saturday morning concerts at the Royal Festival Hall in London. My appreciation of classical music began there, listening to the works of Tchaikovsky, Grieg, Rachmaninov and Holst and to this day, my love of the classics has never faltered. I have to admit that my house is rarely silent as I listen to music throughout the day and it is selected to accompany whatever I am doing. I find music comforting, uplifting and inspiring, on a par with the pleasure one has from reading a good novel and wanting to read more from that particular author. There is music to fit all moods and situations and in my view, life would be bereft without it.

Ralph McTell is the creator of many beautiful songs, the majority written now with a religious theme, but it all began for him with the memorable "Streets of London". How can one listen and not be moved by such poignant words?

Chris Rea also wrote a brilliant piece some ten years ago about a young boy whose Italian immigrant father struggled to make a living in England producing and selling ice-cream. Rea puts the child's hopes and dreams – to be more successful – to music, and in doing so created a unique and successful mini-opera.

Likewise Sir Paul McCartney who co-wrote "She's Leaving Home" with John Lennon, years later penned the impressive and unforgettable "Liverpool Oratorio" with Carl Davis. For someone who cannot write music but only hear it in his head, the talented Mc Cartney, here in my view, created an orchestral masterpiece.

However, we shouldn't dismiss the great Lonnie Donnegan and Humphrey Llyttleton whose skiffle and jazz music of the fifties dominated the airways and paved the way for Elvis Presley, the King of Rock and Roll, and the fore-runner to all musical genre that is popular today.

Various classic standards interpreted by Frank Sinatra Tony Bennett and Barbara Streisand transcend time and bring a great deal of joy to the listener. However much one appreciates their talent, the likes of Michael Jackson, Sir Elton John and Celine Dion will also take their place in musical history as will The Who, Oasis, The Rolling Stones and Abba.

When occasionally we are away from home, I am inevitably drawn into a church to spend a few minutes in silence, take in the atmosphere and wonder how such a beautiful and often intricate building was constructed all those years ago with the simplest of tools available. Did those who built such a masterpiece of architecture work in silence, I wonder - or were they influenced by the music and hymns and of their day, singing whilst they laboured?

Composers of music and lyrics, like authors and poets, have been inspired to put pen to paper by a thought that in turn created a story in words and music. We have a duty to encourage and treasure its art form.

JC

MOIRA DE BLANCA

The blossom was uncurling on the delicate branches, sunlight filtering through on to the dusty street as she came out of the hotel. Coffee aromas tempted her to stop, but no, she had to complete the task she'd set herself. Striding confidently along the wide pavement on legs like stilts, her blackbird hair gleaming in the sun, she caught admiring male glances. In her purple handbag was the address and diving in to find the crumpled piece of paper, she compared it to the name of the square she found herself in. Placa Catalinya and just in that far corner was the Cafe Zurich. Yawning waiters were opening the shutters after the afternoon siesta and a tousled-haired boy was lazily washing the table tops. The clock sang out its melodious chimes - five o'clock. She had plenty of time before the next meeting.

   Suddenly she felt afraid. Twenty nine years she had waited for this moment, since she was two years old. Just what might she discover? And what if her hopes disappeared as quickly as that smear of water rapidly drying on the metal table she found herself leaning against? Its warm solidity reassured her. Drawing herself up to her full impressive height, she fumbled in her bag for her sunglasses. No need of them really as the sun had lost its desperate midday glare and was mellowing in the late spring afternoon. But they made her feel anonymous, less conspicuous, able to peruse faces without the owner being aware of her curious stare.

   Down a cobbled alleyway she went, the gangling houses almost meeting above and the sun struggling to touch the shabby doors and the anaemic plants on windowsills. Number seventeen - she counted carefully as many were numberless - there was nine, twelve, fifteen, then without warning, she found herself staring at a tiny courtyard. There was no house where seventeen should be, just this small area where the sun suddenly poured in and the houses either side formed painted walls. At the back was a tall windowless building as the third side. Nothing! No house, no people to ask, no answers. The silence swirled around her, beating rhythmically in her ears. As she stood there she felt a warm softness brush against her bare leg - a black cat slithered round her, looking hopefully up with piercing emerald eyes. Its pink tongue protruded gently from its mouth and a loud purr broke the sleepy silence.

Is this where it had happened? Had the house never been rebuilt? Bending to stroke the cat, her mind raced with questions. Was there no-one around who could help her?

The door of the house on the left opened suddenly. A frail old man shuffled out, brushing his fingers together as he summoned the cat. His face looked as though it had lived a thousand years, the skin was so wrinkled and brown. The cat abandoned her and ambled to the source of food, treacherously transferring its affection.

'Excuse, signor,' she said hesitantly. 'Casa?' As she asked the question she waved her hand at the courtyard which suddenly, menacingly, lost its warm appearance as the sun slipped behind a cloud.

'Eh?' The old man peered suspiciously at her. Then, without saying a word, he ushered the cat inside and clicked the door firmly closed. Alone again, she wandered into the courtyard; just cobbles, the painted walls and - what was that? A small board stuccoed into the wall at the back. Her Spanish was not good, but scrabbling her dictionary from her bag, she flipped over the pages to translate the stark text.

'Mort.........1979.........Trez.........Basque.........ETA.'

Certain words leapt out, singeing into her mind. Memories stabbed through her like red hot needles. Dark. Noise. A bitter smell. Silence. Then the wailing, the high-pitched agony that would be with her for ever. Tears were running down her face, silent rivers of pain. Impatiently she wiped them away. Standing still for a moment, it was as if something was fluttering in her heart. Should she have tried to revive the past? Was it a desperate mistake? Wasn't it safer to leave it asleep?

Turning abruptly, she walked quickly away from the ghosts of the empty courtyard, back to the spring sunshine, the warmth of people and the living future.

JS

PAVAROTTI DIED TODAY

Pavarotti died today,
they announced it on radio four.
Pancreatic cancer gave him no choice,
a malignant disease killed that voice.

The three tenors are now two
between them, a bearded void.
Nessun dorma bereft of its host,
after Luciano gave it his most.

So farewell great maestro.
White hankie, black beard, beaded brow.
He has performed his greatest opera,
he has taken his greatest bow.

BH

LAKE DISTRICT

Lake District, National Trust, inextricably bonded,
Where walkers carve motorways across the fell sides,
And that host of golden daffodils still dance the
morning breeze.

Dry stone walls purposely meander,
Wainwright still climbs Haystacks,
And the lapping plain chant of water,
Sees Gondola steam upon a watery grave.

66 brings tourists filling dwellings from slate scoured hills,
While Catbells overshadows Moot hall like wad and pencils.

Herdwick laughs at Hardknott
1 in 3s, 1 in 4s mock the faint-hearted.

Waterfalls in coruscating ribbons of beauty
Flooding villages
Quenching Manchester's thirst,
While the ancient symphonic landscape feeds hungry eyes.

RJ

CRAG RAT

The storm fell on them like a tidal wave crashing onto rocks. They were on the narrowest part of the ridge, 2000 feet up and with sheer drops either side.

The wind began to howl and torrential rain soaked them. Richard could only squint at the ground in front of him, and they both fell to one knee. Richard felt his hands slipping from the ridge and signalled and shouted to Paul to lie down below the top. The path was only wide enough for them to lie sideways facing the rock.

The wind increased in ferocity and the rain struck horizontally hitting the top of the ridge and ricocheting off like bullets. The wind blew until it became a screaming demon tearing at him. He felt cold and his fingers ached as he gripped the rock. He saw Paul look back, his face was ashen and his mouth a dark slit. Richard felt fear grip him and he felt its long gnarled fingers enter his abdomen and twist his intestines.

They could not move back and raising any part of the body above the parapet was to invite certain death. How much longer could he hold his grip on the rock? Was this it? Was this to be death? This can't be fair; not only had he killed himself he had probably killed Paul too.

Richard and Paul worked together at a small law firm in London. Richard came back as often as possible to Cumbria, his birthplace, to visit family and walk and climb in the mountains. Paul was a city dweller who scoffed at anything rural and often accused Richard of, "Going off to sit on a hill picking daisies." Richard took most of the sarcasm in good spirit but last week had been different. Paul had looked up from his laptop and said, "It says here the locals in Cumbria call hill walkers, 'Crag Rats'."

"Yes I know," Richard replied, knowing there would be more to come.

Paul leaned back in his seat and put his hands behind his head, " That's it then, you're known as 'Crag Rat' from now on. Don't forget to bring back some daisies at the weekend."

"There are some dangerous and difficult climbs in those mountains," Richard replied.

Their boss had now entered the office and the typists had started to look interested...

"There are some over 3000 feet high," Richard said.

"I'll tell you what," Paul said, " You take me with you at the weekend and may be I'll believe you. Who knows, I might even take up 'crag ratting' for myself."

Richard knew he only wanted to go so that when they returned he could brag about how easy it had been, but he couldn't back down.

"If you want to meet me up there on Sunday, we'll do it."

"No problemo," Paul announced to the office.

The mountain Richard had in mind had a summit of 3000 feet, approached via a mile long ridge called 'Striding Edge'; the ridge fell away on both sides of the pathway. He felt it would be safe enough for Paul in the right conditions but would be an awe-inspiring experience for him.

Sunday morning he had checked the weather forecast – light winds and some rain, not ideal, but safe enough with the right guidance and equipment. Arriving at the car park he saw Paul's black B.M.W. parked. He saw Paul emerge pulling on a blue Pringle golfing jumper and dropping his car keys into a pair of golfing trousers.

"Afternoon, Sherpa Tensing," he said.

"Jesus, what are you wearing? We're going up a mountain not playing golf."

"This stuff's shower proof," he said, kicking the dirt from his ex-army gardening boots.

"Where's the stuff I told you to hire?"

"I'm not paying out for all that rubbish for an afternoon's walk," he replied.

"Look, the weather can change up there in minutes; I can't take you wearing that clothing."

"I've driven all the way here, it's too late to go on a fashion parade, and if you don't go then I'll go on my own. Where's the exit?" he said, striding away.

Richard watched him and knew he had no choice: his own competitive edge had brought Paul here and he couldn't risk him getting lost or hurt. He pulled an old cagoule from his car, ran after Paul throwing it onto his shoulders.

"Put this on – you'll need it up there."

Richard kept Paul ahead of him as they climbed, Paul's boots sending down rivers of stones with each step he took. Paul looked around at one point and said, "Come on, Tensing, keep up, we don't want to be here all day."

Cheeky b****r, Richard thought, we'll see how he copes crossing the ridge.

They climbed steadily. The rain increased slightly and he could see Paul was sweating and breathing heavily. When they reached a plateau at 2000 feet, they could see the magnificent granite and scree-covered ridge that was Striding Edge. For the first time he saw a look of doubt on Paul's face. Is he going to bottle it? he thought.

"Look you don't have to go; we've done most of it," Richard said.

"How long is it?" he asked.

"Just over a mile; the path runs just below the ridge. It's reasonable here but then gets narrow."

"There looks like some big climbs towards the end."

"The main one is about two hundred feet high called 'The Bad Step' – are you still up for it?" he said, still hoping that Paul was going to turn back.

There was a moment's hesitation before the old Paul appeared again. "If you've done it before it can't be too hard, can it."

It had begun to rain hard now and the wind picked up a little. They moved on towards the summit, the path still wide at this point. He told Paul to lead and then followed close behind.

"You alright, Paul? Just take your time and watch your footing."

"Look mother, no hands," he replied holding his arms out.

They moved along the edge for another thirty minutes and traversed along the narrowest part of the path. Then Richard saw it – a line of black smoke filling the horizon to their left. Richard knew it wasn't smoke, it was a huge storm heading for them.

They now found themselves clinging on for life. Richard ran through the options. They couldn't turn back, they had come too far. They couldn't rise above the edge because the wind would blow them off the mountain. He knew Paul must be cold and soaked because of his inadequate clothing. He knew his own hands felt numb and he couldn't be sure how much longer he could hang on. Then it came to him. 'The Bad Edge'; if they could just reach it they could at least take shelter from the wind and if necessary hold on all night.

He decided to move on his side along the ledge. It was

torturous, slow and painful but it was movement and would get some heat back into him. He edged along, reaching Paul's feet and shouted. Paul peered around under his arm, and looked startled. He signalled and shouted for him to start moving forward. After some hesitation Paul nodded and started to move along the path.

After an age, they reached a point where the path began to turn left, Paul moved forward until only his feet were visible and then in an instant Richard saw the feet disappear over the edge. He heard himself screaming, "No!" But the words froze in his throat. Panicking he went towards the spot where he had last seen Paul. He reached the corner and peered down. He saw some boulders sticking out about twelve feet below him, but no body. As he stared at the boulders he could see marks on the wet surfaces. His mind raced. He must have gone over these too. He began frantically looking for a route down when he heard a voice carried on the wind. He listened again. It was his name.

He looked to his left and saw Paul balancing on an outcrop about 100 feet away and below the path.

"Stay there," he shouted. "Don't b****y move."

Paul looked across and held a cupped hand to his ear then shrugged his shoulders. Richard could see blood running down his face; he wondered how badly hurt he was. He reached Paul and then lowered himself down to the small outcrop.

"Where are you hurting?" he shouted in his ear.

"Everywhere! Nothing broken though, I managed to climb back up here."

Richard looked at the wound. It was only superficial.

"You're b****y lucky. We've got to get to the Bad Step. We can't stay here all night, it's too narrow."

"What do you mean, stay here all night? I'm going home."

He could see Paul was shaking. He took off his coat and motioned to him to swap. After another ten minutes, he looked a little stronger.

"We need to start moving." He pointed to the path above them and Paul nodded. They climbed to the path and crawled as before. The granite 200 foot step loomed ahead. When they reached it the pathway widened and they took shelter. The howl of the wind dropped and the rain stopped peppering their faces. They both sat down, the breath pumping from their lungs and said nothing. After a few minutes Richard spoke.

"Do you still want to get off tonight?"

"Yes, of course I do, I want to get off and never b****y comeback," Paul replied.

"Well we can't go over the step; the wind is still too strong. The only other way is to go around it and I've never tried that before."

"Then let's try it now," Paul replied, wiping blood from his face.

"I'll lead. Face the rock and hold with both hands. If I think it's too dangerous, I'll tell you to go back."

"Don't decide that unless you have to," Paul said.

Richard stood up and moved off. Edging forward, clinging to the rock, there was no path now just uneven boulders and scree. After five minutes he looked back at Paul. As he turned his head back his right foot slipped and he landed on his knee, crying out in pain.

"Keep your eyes on the road, you prat," Paul shouted.

They eventually made it through without further incident. They were well below the ridge now which had continued to rise above them. Richard stopped.

"We can go up to the path or we can go down the slope and stay clear of the wind," he said.

"I'm not having anything to do with going up. Down is the only way for me."

"You can see all the rocks and shingle, don't get cocky."

They clung to the mountainside, slipping and sliding sometimes on all fours, sometimes on their backside. They arrived at the bottom exhausted and lay on their backs filthy, their clothes in shreds.

After a few minutes Richard asked, "Do you believe there are mountains in Cumbria now?"

"Look, I never want to talk about this again. When we get back, you don't tell them how stupid I was and I won't tell them how you nearly killed us, all right?"

BH

THE LAST MISSION

Fred Thomas looked out the window – the sun was shining brightly and there wasn't a cloud in sight. John, his only son, had promised to take him to visit the air museum at East Buckton the home of "Sally Ann," a Second World War Lancaster bomber. Fred loved going back there.

During the war East Buckton had been home to several squadrons of Lancaster bombers. Fred, as a young airman, had served as a mid-turret gunner in one of them, flying on countless missions while based there, so every visit brought back memories.

Bang on time John arrived. Betty, his mother, had the door open long before he reached it. Quietly he asked her if his father had taken his medication. Sadly Fred had been diagnosed with Alzheimer's disease two years previously; the medication was controlling the symptoms most of the time. Occasionally he would forget to take the tablets and would become confused and hard to care for. After being told Fred had taken them, he walked into the hall where his father stood waiting.

He could see his eighty-four-year-old father was looking forward to the trip out. "What's kept you?" his father asked, going on to tell John how he had been ready and waiting for almost an hour.

As they walked to his car John noticed how much frailer his father had become in the weeks since his last visit. He felt he owed it to his mother to give her a break from looking after him.

With Fred safely belted in his seat, John started the engine. Looking across at his father's feet he could see them

going through the motions of driving, depressing the clutch and accelerator. He knew how much Fred missed not being allowed to drive.

Fred had held a clean driving licence for more than sixty years. It had almost broken his heart, when with the onset of the Alzheimer's, the doctor had told him he must surrender it.

Within an hour of departing they reached their destination. John was surprised at the speed his father mustered as they made their way to the hanger that housed "Sally Ann."

Fred's excitement grew when he saw a tractor being coupled to the front of the aircraft in readiness to pull her out onto the runway. "I think we've picked a good day to come," John told him after inquiring if they would be starting the engines up.

Having been told that it would be about an hour before they would be ready to run the Rolls Royce engines John suggested they should take a look at some new additions to the collection of wartime memorabilia. Deeply engrossed in the collection he said o.k. when Fred said he was off to visit the gents. When his father failed to return after about fifteen minutes John set off to find him. On checking the toilets he found no trace of his father. Worried he started to search around the aerodrome's remaining buildings.

Fred, after visiting the toilets had started walking down the runway retracing steps he had taken sixty-six years previously. Without a hat the sun's heat caused him to become light-headed. Walking along his body started to shake when in the distance he heard "Sally Ann's" engines burst into life.

Drifting up the runway to meet him were thick patches

of sea-fret blown inland by the easterly wind. Soon he found himself enveloped in them. Listening to the sound of the engines he imagined he was on-board a Lancaster returning from a bombing raid.

Sweat started running from his brow when he heard one engine then a second begin misfiring. Remembering the last time he had heard similar sounds set his heart racing. It was on the last mission he had flown. They had met an almost impenetrable wall of flak as they were approaching their target. Somehow they had managed get through it and drop their bombs despite the flak ripping many holes in the aircraft's fuselage.

The homeward flight had been a nightmare; forced to fly low, mist had seeped in through every rip in the fabric. Worse was still to come. As they neared their base, black smoke replaced the mist, making breathing almost impossible.

Fred re-lived it all, the landing, the bang as the plane's under-carriage collapsed, the fire that appeared on the wings as one engine after another burst into flames. The cries from Sam Roberts, their navigator, as the inferno started to engulf him; the look on his face when Fred had to leave him trapped there and flee to save his own life. Fred still bore the scars where the flames had burnt his arms and legs as he had tried to free Sam.

He and Jim Brown, the tail gunner, were the only members of the crew to survive. Jim had managed to escape despite having his arm broken in the crash. They had remained good friends until Jim's death, never mentioning the war or the crash.

Fred stood and listened when the sounds of the engines stopped. In the mist he tasted smoke and began panicking. Further into the mist he stumbled, the smoke's acrid taste getting stronger with each step he took. Then he saw it – a large fire in the midst of which he saw a figure dressed in a flying suit.

Without thinking he rushed forward, grabbed the man's shoulder and pulled with every ounce of strength he could muster.

Gasping for breath he somehow managed to drag the man and himself clear of the fire before collapsing.

Half-an-hour later, when the mist had cleared, the crew on board "Sally Ann" spotted them as she taxied down the runway.

The Lancaster had hardly stopped when they jumped out and ran the hundred yards or so to where Fred lay.

Sadly they were too late; Fred lay dying from the heart attack brought on by his heroic actions. With great difficulty he'd asked if Sam was alive and safe.

At his inquest, it was revealed that the man in the old flying suit was in fact a scare-crow who the birds had become accustomed to. The farmer having found other means of frightening them, had placed him on the pile of rubbish, ready to burn when the wind blew in the right direction. Unfortunately when he lit the bonfire the wind unexpectedly changed.

To Betty and John, Fred died a hero. Was the look on Sam's face still haunting him after all those years or was there another reason why he did what he did? Who will ever know?

GB

*The following three poems were 'commissioned' by RAF
Waddington and will be used by them in the Freedom of
Lincoln celebrations in April.*

SENTRY

For Faith and Freedom
The station motto entreats,
Aircraft stand on sentry
A warning drum to beat.

Operational over 92 years
The airfield has maintained,
Through Lancaster to Boeing,
Waddington has remained.

At night her runway and tracks
Illuminated red, orange and green;
Each colour has its meaning,
Each a reason to be seen.

A self-contained town,
Schools, shops and opportunity.
A powerful arm of the military,
A giving hand to community.

So when you next drive by the base,
Give a thought to what goes on there –
Guarding the western world
From an evil that might just dare.

BH

FAITH AND FREEDOM

Spies from the sky slumber
Where touchdown meets trunk road,
V force member recalls times from the past.
Perimeter fence halts stepladder army,
While faith and freedom holds Lincoln's keys.

Ambucopter scrambles,
Airmen's boots crash on tarmac.
Blasts walls redundant, cold war no longer looms.
Chequered caravan guards landing and take off,
While faith and freedom still holds Lincoln's keys.

Hangars for housing,
Runway lights for safe landing.
Airshow attracts from near and afar.
Police dogs guard ninety-year history,
While faith and freedom forever holds Lincoln's keys.

RJ

AIR FORCE BLUES...

A 21st Century sonnet as a tribute to RAF Waddington

Here in the heart of Lincolnshire,
for years the resonant sound of guardians
of our land has echoed through the skies.
This vast flat ground is scored with runway roads,
haunted by shadows of past planes that flew;
from training craft that soared into the blue
to practise circuits here, to heavy Lancs.
droning their loads so far away, their stoic crew
protecting us, to mighty roar from Vulcan's
powerful thrust. And now our trust
depends on eyes fixed fast on future goals.
Three thousand souls unite to help defend
the freedom of our world. They spread support,
engender faith and strive to reach for heights
and stars with ardour, strength and right.

Faith and Freedom.
Per Ardua ad Astra

JS

EYESORES ON OUR STREETS

Is there no end in sight
To those boards that appear overnight,
After estate agents have answered the call
To sell houses large and small?
Insensitive to where they're placed
Badly erected and tightly spaced;
Some are plain on a simple post
While others colourful designs host.
'For sale, for sale,' the words stand out.
'Sold,' is something they rarely shout,
For potential buyers have long gone
Leaving them precariously hanging on,
Hoping that they can stand the strain
Of further months in the sun and rain,
To creak and flap in the breeze
While property investors cough and wheeze
At the thought of a credit crunch
And smaller portions for their business lunch.

GB

SECRETS OF THE TIDE

If the tide could speak what tales it would tell
Of mighty seas where mariners set sail,
Of universal explorers and travellers ships
Constantly battling the wild tempest.

If the tide could speak what tales it would tell
Of hurricane winds and the hail-stoned air.
The mighty sea-world above and beneath
Murky secrets forever to keep.

If the tide could speak what tales it would tell
Of shipwrecks beneath that mighty swell,
And lives painfully buried within that foul bed
Whilst hungry seagulls swoop overhead.

If the tide could speak what tales it would tell
Of seafaring warriors who fought battles brave,
Whilst mountains of waters surged in their midst
When Death showed them a door they couldn't resist.

If the tide could speak what tales it would tell
Of raging storm clouds battering the swell,
Where deep below those powerful waves
Rest brave sailors in their sea-bed graves.

JC

REGRETS

He stands watching the encroaching tide
Destroying sandcastles, built with pride,
Its creeping water edged with foam
Finds shallow gullies into which to roam.
Thinking if only he could take that tide,
And use it to hide his crime.
For drink, the devil's brew
Had him in its grip before he knew.
Was it the ten pints or more
That flushed common-sense out the door?
A push or shove led to the fight,
Him striking out with all his might;
Never will he forget that sound
When his opponent hit the ground.
The red blood that gushed from the head,
His panic upon realising he was dead.
Disappearing into the night
Body shaking, filled with fright.
Exhausted he slept the night away,
Waking to the cold light of day,
His mind a whirling murky pool
Its one clear thought, "You are a fool,
If only you had had less to drink
You may have been able to stop and think."
Now while he waits for the men in blue
His life he starts to review;
Last night before he become de-ranged
Was there something he could have changed?
That taste of the devil's brew
Was only meant to be a glass or two
But after they had been swallowed deep

Away from the bar he couldn't keep.
Now faced with time in a prison cell,
Will life become a living hell?
Twelve by eight feet of depressive space
Shared with another misfit of the human race,
Twenty-four hours in which to sit and stew
And wish he had never tasted the devil's brew.

GB

CELEB

Celebrity is the thing to be, right here,
right now, in this century.
You can be a chef, you can be a singer
you can be famous just as a Blinger.

Be a millionare for baring your chest,
While patients wait on the N.H.S.
T.V and Magazines are your scene,
Just hide the poverty in between.

Books and Biographies by ghost writers,
Cook in Hells Kitchen, while tramps are
burnt with lighters.
Yeh, you got it made if you're on Big Brother,
The more bigoted and cruel you are to each other.

So here's to Celebrity, in this Century,
A world without substance, where ignorance means gain,
And the worthless are celebrated during fifteen minutes
of fame.

BH

THIS GREEN AND
PLEASANT LAND

Beryl spread her large body in the middle of the
front row, determined to have the best seat. Jolly
uncomfortable it was too, sitting on a chair designed for an
eleven year old. Not that she was fat, just well-built as her
mother used to say, piling more mashed potato on her
plate. Mum was long gone, resting in the little churchyard
only yards from the Church School where Beryl was
caretaker. Still smelling of disinfectant, chair creaking in
sympathy, she heaved an enormous sigh as she thought of
the sixty plus years she'd lived in this village - and the
dreaded changes about to be forced on them.

'You're early,' sang out a cheerful voice as Annie swung
through the door and plonked down next to her. 'Thought
I'd be first.' Annie's house had survived demolishment
when they'd built the by-pass thirty years ago but it meant
she lived within feet of thunderous traffic on the dual-
carriageway that roared past her front windows. Stubbornly
both ladies clung to the measurements they knew and
understood, refusing to 'Measure in Metric' as the latest
slogan ordered. Both were well over sixty but still hard at
work – no-one got a state pension until they were seventy
in the year 2012.

'Hello, you two.' Another large elderly lady joined them
causing the three to flow over five chairs. Unfortunately all
the folding wooden chairs so comfortably accommodating
to adult bottoms had been sold off when the new purpose-
built school-community-hall had been finished and the
beautiful wooden village hall that had fallen foul of Health
and Safety, demolished as a fire hazard.

'Hello, Vera. You've shut up shop early today.'

'Well it was nearly seven so hoped no-one would notice.'

'Just hope it wasn't that vixen from the pub. She'd report you as soon as look at you, bad-tempered wretch.'

As they continued to gossip and fidget, the school hall gradually filled up.

Promptly at eight an assorted group of people self consciously ambled forward and faced the packed room. Voices faded. Everyone waited in anticipation.

'Evenin', members of Community Sixty Seven, District Twenty Two of Region Five.' The words were uttered in a rich local accent. 'Welcome and thank you for coming out this chilly Autumn night.' The heavily built speaker stopped, lowered his voice, 'and in half an hour our Local European officer will be joining us.' A sound like a hiss spun round the room followed by a cacophony of coughs. 'To-night,' continued the florid faced farmer, 'we have to look at our latest - um - edict.' He peered at a piece of paper, fumbling with his spectacles as he tried to read it.

Cathy sat at the back of the hall, watching those large red hands as they clutched the information. How many times had she prised those fingers off her arm, brushed those wandering hands away and firmly refused to engage in any familiarity with his lordship. He wasn't really a lord, just his nickname in the village but he seemed to think he had manorial rights over any vulnerable female; for generations the Pedwardines had lived in The Manor farming the land for miles around and most families had been employed by them until 2007, the year that England died. Cathy remembered that day in October when the Scottish Prime Minister had signed away their nation to Brussels. Waving a piece of paper as he landed at Heathrow, his words, 'The Treaty is signed' were reminiscent of a previous Prime Minister in 1939, she thought. Perhaps it was only justice

that on Burn's Night the following year a haggis thrown at him by a kilt-wearing Scotsman shouting 'Gorrrdon, weer's yer kilt?' had knocked him out so thoroughly that when he came round he'd imagined he was Rabbie Burns and tried to speak in rhyme all the time. Quietly retired six months later, whichever political party was in charge found they had very little control over matters anyway. Brussels ruled.

'Wrong glasses? Shall I read it for you?' The question came from another gentleman, taller, slimmer and more urbane than the weatherbeaten farmer. He just had wandering eyes but between the two there seethed a silent rivalry, as each struggled to become the most influential powerful alpha male in the village. Roland Parker, who had only lived in the place for fifteen years, took the paper from Ben Pedwardine's hands with a smile of satisfaction.

A humming silence as everyone held their breath, then

'Well, we know that our gardens are under threat, don't we?' So the rumours were true. 'Anyone who owns more than twenty fee – I mean, metres of land deemed non-agricultural must forfeit that land for newbuild in order to accommodate newcomers.' This was a euphemism for all the people who had poured into this green and pleasant land only to turn it into one massive congested red-brick sprawl, and who now outnumbered the indigenous population by two to one. 'Any persons resisting will be forced to take another requisitioned family into their home in addition to losing their land.'

Sitting as near to Cathy as he dared, Jack watched her covertly. Although they both worked in the school, she as secretary and he as a teacher, they didn't have much socialising at work. Coming into teaching after fifteen years in banking, Jack was entranced with the job and the school. Looking out over green fields dotted with sheep, enthusing ten-year-olds with a thirst for knowledge, contrasted so vividly with the grey city and financial greed he'd been used to that he couldn't believe his luck. More so when he first saw Cathy; a young widow, neat, pretty, a shadow of sadness clinging to her, she worked part-time in the office.

There was a bustle in the front and a heavily-breathing body suddenly obscured everyone's view as Beryl heaved herself to her feet. 'That's not possible!' Her loud voice used to admonishing children to 'pick that up now' rang across the hall. 'My garden is my living, what with my chickens, my veggie plot and my cut flowers. Do they expect me to 'ave a bloomin' 'ouse built on it? 'Ow am I expected to make a living?'

'Quite.' Smoothly Ben Pedwardine soothed her ruffled feathers. 'But the reason we're here tonight, Mrs Smith, is to find a way out of this.' He looked round the hall, his eyes resting briefly on Cathy as he waited for a response. It came all at once as comments were shouted over each other and several stood up and began waving arms crossly. 'Order!' he said firmly and gradually the hubbub subsided. 'Now, one at a time. Any positive action we can take?'

There was a silence then Graham, Ben's foreman, stood up and said in a deep slow burr, 'Can't we sabotage the sites, Boss. Stop the b.....s building by wrecking everything nightimes like...?'

Roland stretched his face into a tight smile. 'As an ex-government official, Graham, I have to say all that'll do is get you into trouble. There'll be surveillance cameras for a start, and security night-patrolling. No, we have to think of something more subtle. Any other ideas?'

Frustration and despair was on everyone's face. A brisk punch-up had settled many disputes in the good old days of the nineties, honour satisfied and hands shaken afterwards over a pint in the pub. Rural England had changed; no longer were the people in charge of their own destinies or even everyday lives. No longer could the law be taken into their own hands; the law was thousands of European Directives and the latest one concerned the fact that only a few pastures of green were left across England for animal rearing and crop growing. This meant private land was to be requisitioned to build the endless number of houses needed for the endless number of a rapidly breeding population.

In the gloomy lull that followed a voice spoke. 'There may be a way of invoking an ancient law.'

Eyes focussed like headlamps on the figure of Jack. Who was this newcomer? He hadn't been in the place for two minutes and.....but this was no time for village prejudice, or solidarity as they preferred to call it.

'I've been reading up on our old laws and although the European Articles mainly override them, it may be a way of delaying or confusing them,' he began hesitantly. A murmur of hope ran though the audience. 'I knew he was a clevr'un,' offered Beryl in a satisfied stage whisper. Jack was lodging with her until he could find a place of his own and she took a proprietorial pride in him. 'We can call a poll tonight - all the rules of a Local Government Act of 1972 are in place to "demand one on any question arising at the meeting." If a third of you will vote in favour....'

Before he could finish speaking, Graham stood up again. 'Right,' he roared above the noise, 'I votes we refuse to give up our gardens and evicts any building firm comin' in to the village.'

Every hand in the place shot up. The cheer of approval was cut short as the door opened and a tall thin figure in a grey suit stood importantly in its frame.

'Ah,' Ben hadn't forgotten his manners but struggled to hide his distaste. 'Monsewer, um, Bouissaille, welcome to Merrr - I mean, Community Sixty Seven.'

Fussily the grey-haired, grey-faced man took a laptop from his case and set it on one of the tables at the back. 'Just continue,' he said, then with a look of superiority announced, 'I shall be filling in a report as we go along. I take it you all know why I am here?' Without waiting for a reply, he launched into a much longer version of the edict that Ben and Roland had already described. Then he sat at the laptop and tapped away ominously. From where he sat, Jack could see it was an official form being filled in, the sort of forms he'd spent so many boring years being suffocated by.

Suddenly a look of discomfort crossed M. Bouissaille's face. 'I wonder,' he murmured to Jack, 'is there, er, can I, er, where is....?' Jack understood. 'Mrs Smith,' he called, 'could I have the key to the Staff suite, please?'

Beryl bustled to the back, a waft of cleaning fluid in her wake.

'Well, Mr Brussels,' she said as if talking to a naughty child. 'I'll have to unlock for you. Very unorf'dox this is.' They disappeared through the door and Annie and Vera applied themselves to the tea-urn at the front. Despite the miserable reason for the meeting, the villagers looked forward to a cup and a chat. Jack slipped after Beryl who was waiting outside the Staff block, jangling the bunch of keys that was attached to her like glue.

'Can you delay him for a few minutes, Beryl? I've got an idea.' 'As long as you like, love,' retorted Beryl a salacious gleam in her eye as she put the key in the lock of the staff corridor and turned it. 'Pity I'm a bit deaf, innit?'

Hastily Jack slipped back in the hall. No-one was watching him - or so he thought - as he sat in front of the open computer and surreptitiously tapped in a few details. His hand hovered for a moment over 'send' then the completed form was in cyberspace on its way to the monotonous miles of records in Headquarters, Brussels. Another few taps and the empty form returned as if it hadn't been touched, but Jack knew from experience it couldn't override the information sent.

'What are you doing?' A soft delicious voice whispered in his ear and a soft delicious scent filled his senses, as Cathy leant conspiratorially over his shoulder.

'Just helping,' he murmured as he turned smiling. 'Pity this village doesn't exist anymore. I'd have liked to ask you out this Saturday.' 'Then we'll have to find a non-existent place to go,' was her enigmatic reply.

JS

THE GOLDEN LETTER

A letter hugs the mat.
Stamps bright with flowers
from New Zealand
glow on the blue surface.
As she trembles and tears it open,
photos spill
and a golden picture
fills her world
with sunlight.

There on endless sands
hazy with warmth
sits a family of love,
four of them
so far away
forever
smiling.

Here on a summer day
English rain
smears her sight -
or is it tears,
as she dreams
on the scene
from New Zealand?

JS

MIRRORED IMAGE

Many years ago on holiday I saw
An old lady walking sprightly by the shore.
A weather-beaten face she had
And dressed for the weather she was clad.
With not a care in the world she strode
Along the shore in cheerful mode.
Striding forth she passed me by
A smile on her face and a twinkle in her eye.
And now as I think of her, it is me
Striding out happily beside the sea.

JC

SEPTEMBER MORNING

In the silence of the early morning, Serena slipped from beneath the warm duvet leaving her husband sleeping soundly. She crossed the hall and went into her cosy kitchen. Serena loved the silence of the morning. It was a time when she could gather her thoughts, reflect on memories and then begin to plan the day ahead.

She filled the kettle and stood in silence looking out of the kitchen window. The dawn sky was dull and grey but within the stillness was a beauty which reached her soul.

The boiling kettle broke the silence as she took a mug from the cupboard. Serena made a pot of tea and leaving it to brew she wandered quietly round the bungalow. It felt comforting and safe. The hall clock ticked in unison with the kitchen clock, tick, tick, tick. She passed the bathroom, hearing the drip, drip, drip from the leaking shower-head; a job her husband had promised to do amongst several others for some while now.

She returned to the kitchen and pouring her first mug of tea she walked over with it to sit in her favourite spot at the table where she could view her world from the window.

A cyclist came down the street, his sleepy face taking in the cool morning air. As if to order, the pond pump began to start its work for the day gently moving the water. Beneath the ripples, the fish began to stir from their slumbers, gliding across the cold surface.

The paper boy lumbered by, carrying his heavy bag and probably wishing he was still tucked up under his duvet, oblivious to the world in a deep slumber.

At that moment Sandie, the family cat slithered from the comfort of her cosy bed and rolled across the kitchen rug, beckoning Serena to ruffle her fur. Suddenly, the boiler came to life and the constant hum of the refrigerator was lost within the start of the morning.

A neighbour's car engine could be heard down the street which in turn woke the nearby colony of rooks who began noisily leaving their nesting places squawking loudly as they soared skyward. The watery sun appeared through the early morning cloud. September morn! Serena smiled to herself as the clock chimed loudly. Another day had begun.

JC

AND THEY SEEM SO YOUNG

And they seem so young, they whom
Government send to far off lands.
They who leave their families and loved ones
and risk all in desert sands.

And they seem so young, those that we
watched on the TV last night.
Laden down with equipment, frightened
and confused by the fight.

And they seem so young, they who left their
Countries far behind.
The foreign faces that they see, can smile
for a gift and kill behind the lines.

And they seem so young, those faces we saw on the news.
And they seem so young, the soldiers carrying the coffins
and sitting in the pews.

BH

"THE DEVIL'S BROOD"

Betty Moore knew something was wrong when on entering the small meeting room everyone's eyes focused on her. The other members of the Lower Didcot Writer's Circle were already there talking amongst themselves. Normally she was one of the first to arrive but due to a phone-call was slightly late.

Simon Read, the chairperson of the group, rose to his feet. Holding a magazine in front of him, he began, "Normally I would read out the minutes of our last meeting first but today most of you want to find out how our novel has come to be published in here."

Their novel, "The Devil's Brood", chronicled the lives of a family, some law-biding and pillars of the community, others were serious criminals. The members of the circle had each written a chapter about a member of the family; these stories compiled together made an interesting novel.

Betty turned white when she saw the magazine in Simon's hand. It wasn't a well-known British publication but an American crime magazine which had never appeared in the U.K.

"Someone owes us an explanation," Simon said, staring in Betty's direction. "When we embarked on the project wasn't it agreed that if it went to publication the group would be named as its author? Now only by sheer chance do we find our novel is being serialised in an American publication, with only one member being credited as the author." Rodger Jones, a retired accountant and a founder member of the circle, could hardly wait for Simon to stop speaking before standing to add his penny's worth. "After the time and effort we all devoted to the piece of work in question, it seems to me that trying to write anything further as a group would be pointless if this is what happens."

Jean Richards shook her head as she looked around at her fellow writers, most of who were nodding in agreement with what Rodger had said. "Most of you know that I sit on the local bench. With every case we hear, we have to listen to both the prosecution's and the defence's arguments before passing a judgement. As a close friend of Betty's I think we should hear her explanation before passing judgement," she said, sounding very much like a lawyer for the defence.

Simon leapt to his feet again, scowling in Jean's direction said, "This isn't your courtroom and if you think you can lay the law down here, think again. I'll make sure that Betty gets a fair chance to explain why she did what she did."

Jean looked up, her eyes peering over the glasses that always seemed to be resting right at the end of her nose, her face flushed as she replied, "I'm sorry if I gave that impression. You're right, it's up to you, the chair, to see the matter doesn't get out of hand."

Turning to face Betty, Simon said, "The floor is all yours. I hope you have a good explanation."

Betty looked around at her fellow writers before rising to her feet. "I'm extremely sorry for what has happened. Perhaps if I can explain the circumstances leading to the novel's submission you might temper your judgements," she said with tears starting to well-up in her eyes.

"Several months ago my heating boiler began playing-up. I had the service people out only to be told it's beyond repair and a replacement would cost about two thousand pounds. As I don't have that kind of money I approached my bank for a loan only to be turned down. I also tried several well-known credit companies without success.

"One day whilst looking on the internet I came across that magazine's website. They were inviting submissions, offering to pay good money for any they accepted. After a lot of heart-searching, I foolishly submitted our novel, almost sure that they, like the other publishers, would reject it.

"Much to my surprise I received an e-mail within a week informing me that they had accepted it and would begin its serialisation in their next issue. I thought long and hard about telling you at our last meeting but was too ashamed and frightened to do so."

There was a minute's silence before the members started whispering to each other. Betty, unable to hear what was being said, felt like a prisoner waiting for the jury's return.

"The one thing you didn't mention was how much they paid you. I presume it was only a paltry fee not mega bucks," Rodger Jones asked cynically.

"They paid me one thousand dollars," Betty replied.

"Around five hundred pounds for our story. Unbelievable! That's more than most of us have ever received for a piece of work," Rodger uttered after scribbling some figures on his note pad.

"I suppose you now have a nice new boiler and sit at home snug and warm thanks to all of us," his wife Mary chipped in.

Betty reached into her handbag, pulled out an envelope, out of which she produced a cheque. "No I haven't. This is only the second time I've looked at the cheque since it arrived. My conscience won't let me cash it," she said.

"Well what do propose doing with it then?" Rodger asked.

"I would like to write out a cheque, payable to the circle's bank account when I've banked this one. I know what I did was wrong robbing you all of a chance of fame. Tomorrow I'll e-mail the magazine to see if they'll publish your names as the novel's true authors. This will be the last meeting of the writer's circle I shall be attending. I'm deeply sorry to have let you all down so badly," she replied with tears rolling down her face.

For a moment everyone seemed lost for words. Writer looked to fellow writer for inspiration until out of the far comer of the room came a soft voice.

"I know you think of me as the quiet one of our group as I find speaking in public very hard but for once I'm determined to have my say. Yes, Betty was wrong selling our novel but I applaud her for doing so. After we had spent several months trying various publishers without any success what did we do with our novel? We put it to bed while we argued amongst ourselves where to send it next. At least Betty rightly or wrongly did something positive with it," Sandra Johnson said.

Sandra was one of the founder members of the Lower Didcot Writer's Circle, much respected for her work on behalf of the group.

Simon rose to his feet after Sandra had finished speaking. "I think it would be better for Betty, if she doesn't mind, going into the kitchen to make the tea while we have an open debate on the matter."

Betty, as she neared the kitchen, could hear Rodger's voice calling for her to be banished from the circle. Entering the kitchen she busied herself making the tea and putting the biscuits out onto the plates. Tears kept flowing down her face as she thought about what she had done and what had been said.

After sometime Jean Richard's head appeared around the

door. "Is the tea made yet, Betty?" she asked. "I think everyone's more than ready for a cuppa. Would you please bring the trolley down to the meeting room when you're ready?"

Pushing the trolley in front of her Betty made her way back. As she poured out the tea she could feel the tension in the room. Some smiled when saying thank you, while others remained stony faced.

After everyone had finished their drinks, Simon turned to Betty. "While you were out of the room we held a ballot to see whether we wanted you to remain a member of the circle. The outcome of which showed that the majority of us would like you to stay," he said.

Betty, having already made the decision to leave, thought carefully before replying. "I'm deeply moved that so many of you want me to remain in the group after what I've done, but not wanting to cause anymore friction between friends, this will be my last meeting. Once again, before I leave, can I again say how sorry I'm for what has happened?"

As she left Betty knew that through her foolishness, like the family in the group's novel "The Devil's Brood," the writer's circle would be divided for a long time to come.

GB

FIRE AND ICE

Fire and ice,
husband and wife.
But who is the fire,
and who is the ice?

Ice cools the fire,
fire warms the ice.
But who is the fire,
and who is the ice?

Ice loves the fire,
fire loves the ice
But who is the fire,
and who is the ice?

Ice can be fire,
fire can be ice.
Now who is the fire
and who is the ice?

RJ

And a seventh voice.....!

Dr. Richard Shaw, archaeological lecturer and writer, was one of the original members; he disappeared on his archaeological travels but returned in time to include the following two fascinating articles. An impressive academic background reflects his world-wide knowledge and experience and we are privileged to include these contributions.

Ice crystals in entrace to adit, Port Radium, Great Bear Lake

ICE AND FIRE

The Twin Otter flew north out of Alberta and into the North West Territories of Canada. For hour after hour we passed over endless configurations of lakes and trees with occasional rocky ridges. There were no settlements or signs of man. I contemplated about where we were headed. It was the early 1970s and a few days before I had been walking the streets of Edmonton looking for work and had gone into the Chamber of Mines where I had been offered a job at Echo Bay Mines. I was shown a map. Echo Bay Mines is a long way north, located at Port Radium on the east side of Great Bear Lake just below the Arctic Circle.

Arriving at Port Radium was like coming to a long lost northern settlement. Great Bear Lake is vast, about two hundred miles across from west to east and has the longest coastline of any lake in the world. The eroded rounded rocks on the eastern shore are some of the most ancient rocks found on earth. A jutting finger of rock points into the lake and on this is situated Port Radium with a conglomeration of white wooden buildings with stairways up the rocky sides and between the buildings. It is only a mining settlement with about sixty people living there, miners - a few with wives, millworkers, workers in the mess and office, and there is even a post office.

I started work in the mess but soon changed to the mill, where I filled huge cardboard boxes with black dust of silver, lead, and zinc ore. The boxes were on rail cars which I pushed out into a sidings. It was a very dirty job and the ore dust became embedded in the lines of my hands. Then it was summer and in the evenings I loved to walk by the lake which I called the sea as it was like one. It was light until midnight and you could be out at ten o'clock in the evening in bright sunshine. You had to be careful if the breeze ceased because then you could be attacked by blackflies, who left painful bites that would swell and itch unbearably for days. Some people are allergic to their bites and may need to be flown out. I changed to work in the primary crusher where rock from the mine was tipped by truck on to a grizzly, a mesh of bars, and then was broken up by a powerful crusher. Some rocks were too big to go through the grizzly and I had to break them up with a fourteen pound hammer. The resulting rocky ore dropped into an underground cavern - the orepass - from where it went by conveyor belt out of the mountain and through a series of steps into the mill. This was the secondary crusher and there I worked for the rest of my time at Port Radium.

In the mill was a great ball mill that pulverised the ore into a fine powder for the flotation process. On Midsummer's Day the ball mill broke down and to my delight I was given the day off. I went exploring along the lake, finding beautiful secret wildflower gardens in sheltered niches that no other human eye had seen or was likely to see. The rocks are carpeted in juniper and tiny trees that spread out at the base to avoid the wind. Larger trees grow against the side of low south facing cliffs.

Great Bear Lake has the world record lake trout of sixty-five pounds and the north shore of the lake has an exclusive fishing lodge with rich fishermen coming from all over the world. It was these lake trout that sustained Captain John Franklin and his expediton of 1825-27 when he wintered at the western side of the lake, at Fort Franklin, which is now the main settlement on Great Bear Lake. I sent home to England for my Hardy spinning rod, which weighs less than four ounces. I caught several trout from the shore and then one evening I fished into a deep hole from where a thirty-five pounder had been caught. I thought the line had snagged the bottom but then realised I had hooked a big fish. For five minutes I didn't see it, then I gradually played it to the edge and took it out, a magnificent trout about twelve pounds. I would have liked a photo to send to my brother but had no camera. I called out to a boat in the lake but they didn't hear what I said and just waved. It takes six years for a fish to grow one pound in Great Bear Lake. I wondered how old this fish was and decided I wasn't going to kill it and take it to the settlement just for its picture - I'm a vegetarian so wouldn't eat it - and so I let it go back into the lake. That was the last time I ever went fishing.

As August progressed and the water cooled the fish went into deeper water. Fall comes briefly in the first week of September with lovely shades of red in the ground dwelling plants. Soon after the first snow fell and this was to stay on the ground with other light falls for the next six months. The lake started to freeze over. The long Arctic winter was setting in. The temperature kept falling and before long it was too cold to go for walks. I found this out to my cost one day when I went for a walk on the frozen lake in snowshoes. It was twenty below and on getting back it took me a long time to get warm. By December we were living in a twilight world with the red glow of a sunrise immediately followed by the sunset. The sun never came over the horizon. It was like a distant volcanic eruption. The lake continued to freeze over until it was several feet thick and the planes landed on a cleared ice runway. By the shore it was as though waves had frozen in mid flight with panes of ice at all angles. Further out there were lines of pressure ridges where currents pushed the ice against the shore. These were awe-inspiring to see with massive blocks of glistening blue ice broken and forced vertically upward. By January the temperature was minus forty degrees Fahrenheit and sometimes fifty below. I knew it was minus fifty when an ice fog formed around the buildings. Coming to early breakfast at six a.m. after night shift I passed the man taking the weather readings and he told me the temperature.

Some nights I was working alone in the crusher house, the stepped buildings of which came out of the hillside. It was fifty below and a fifty mile an hour wind was blowing from the icy lake and buffeting the buildings. Each shift I had to walk down the long tunnel with the conveyor belt that brought ore from the orepass to check all was well.

The tunnel went into the mountain. This was supposed to be haunted. One night before I worked there the secondary crusher operator came down into the mill white as a sheet and said he had seen a ghost down the long tunnel. The next day he quit and flew out. Towards the end of the tunnel you walked over a trapdoor beneath which a passage led to the underground workings of the mine. There were seventy-five miles of tunnels beneath the lake and cement was constantly used to stop the water getting in. As I walked down the long tunnel in the middle of the night, when I came to the trapdoor I stamped my boot on it and said 'Hello ghost!' At the top of the conveyor belt when I was bringing ore along it I had to sit and look out for chunks of native silver, more than seventy per cent solid silver, which would smash the crushers, and take them off the belt. If the rock was dry, the endless variety of colours of the minerals was a breathtaking sight. I had to wear a radiation badge to monitor for radiation, and the badges were sent once a month to Ottawa to be checked. In 1930 the prospector Gilbert LaBine discovered pitchlende at the entrance to Echo Bay. Pitchblende was processed into radium which had vital uses in medicine and fetched enormous prices on the world market. Silver and copper were also found. This sparked a mining rush to Great Bear Lake and was the start of Port Radium. In the 1930s the dangers of radiation were not fully known and most of those who worked in the mine at Port Radium died when they were young, including the father of a Canadian friend. When I worked there the mine was not producing uranium but silver, lead, and zinc. However, there was still a danger from radon gas and huge fans were installed underground to disperse this. Once I went down into the mine. Huge cracks at different angles kept apart by timbers had been cut by miners as they followed veins of silver. Never again would I look at silver jewellery worn by women without thinking of the colossal work involved in obtaining this precious metal. Down one remote tunnel reached from the trapdoor in the orepass tunnel miners discovered a supply of huge chunks of native silver and nearby were several copies of Playboy magazine. It seemed as though some worker had hidden the silver there and sat dreaming of how he would spend his riches. There was only one snag, how to get the silver out of Port Radium. So the thief left his silver hoard and his dream behind when he left. Legitimately, large pieces of native silver were sealed in small drums and flown out.

In late January the sun emerged after a month of greyness and it was dazzling and overwhelming. One day the temperature went up to minus ten and we were outside rolling up our sleeves! It was like a heatwave. For months we had only been able to go dressed in parkas along the walkways from building to building. Now we could pause and admire the view over to Mystery Island and across the frozen lake. One day coming from the mess with Tom, the Irish mill mechanic, we stopped to look over the lake and he pointed out six dots on the horizon. Were they caribou or trucks ? We waited and after a while as the dots enlarged we saw tiny puffs of steam from the vertical exhausts of trucks. They were bringing in great bladders of fuel for the power station. The lead truck had a huge snowplough at the front. When they encounter pressure ridges they may need to use dynamite to blast a way through.

Gradually we were able to take short walks away from the camp. In the mill worked a young Finn who had brought cross-country skis with him and when he was on night shift he started going out skiing in the afternoons. One day he came to see me in a state of great excitement and said there was something he had found he wanted to show me. He wouldn't say what it was. The snow was thin enough to be able to walk over it and we made our way across the white landscape to some rocky bluffs. In the snowy side of the hillside I could see a hole had been made in the snow covered ice. This was what the Finn wanted to show me. He said to go through the hole. I could see it was the entrance to an old adit – a horizontal tunnel – of the mine but it had been transformed during the long winter. The ceiling and sides were a mass of giant ice crystals a foot or more in length. The floor was ice with icy stalagmites formed here and there and also close to the sides. Free of ice the adit would have been about six feet high. It was a sight of rare beauty formed over months of intense cold in the darkness of this tunnel.

This adit must have been one of the early workings of the mine. It might have been one of those dating from the Second World War. Then this area of Great Bear Lake became a secret zone controlled by the American military. No longer was radium used solely for medical healing. Uranium was being used to develop an atomic bomb at Los Alamos in New Mexico. The uranium used for the atomic bombs dropped on Hiroshima and Nagasaki came from the mine at Port Radium.

As I gazed in wonder at the ethereal ice crystals of the adit I wondered if the uranium for these bombs came from this very tunnel. How could this destruction come from a place of such tranquillity and beauty. It was man who had caused the metamorphosis of the rock.

The Finn and I marvelled in silence and then walked quietly down the hillside.

RS

COMMUTING IN MUMBAI

It was February 2000 and I was on an Emirates jet bound for India on a research expedition to find carvings of ascetics on temples following the completion of my Ph.D. The partitions in the plane were great images of sand dunes in the desert and gazing on these at 30,000 feet seemed rather out of context. We landed at Mumbai – the name now for Bombay – at 2 am and I joined a fellow Englishman in a taxi to Colaba Causeway where the hotels are near the sea and the Gateway to India. Jeremy had come to India for only three days on a 'jolly' as he called it to a Parsi ritual celebration with friends he had met on a previous visit to India. The Parsis, from 'Persians,' are Zoroastrians who settled on the west coast of India from the eighth century. In Mumbai one passes their fire temples, for fire is thought of as purifying in essence and is ritually tended. Exposure of the dead on Towers of Silence is a declining practice. It is said that Indian vultures are not aggressive enough and so vultures were brought from Persia!

I bought a train ticket for Abu Road in Rajasthan to visit the Jain temples at Mt Abu. A tourist officer had told me it would be best to catch the train at Borivale, a suburban station on the edge of Mumbai. This was not a good idea as I was to find out. Even though I left in mid-afternoon to avoid the rush hour, the train out from the centre to Borivale became so packed I struggled to look after my luggage. Arriving at Borivale I discovered that there is no waiting room and an endless procession of trains disgorge and engorge thousands of commuters. On one platform I saw a dead body covered in a white sheet with a pool of blood under the head. At a place set back a little from the passing throng were a French woman and her eleven year old son sitting on a cloth, who invited me to join them. They were going to Pushgar, a sacred city in Rajasthan. During their three months in India they had been robbed and experienced many adventures. They were waiting for the same train, which didn't arrive until nine in the evening, five hours away. Finding straps on my sandals coming loose I sought a roadside cobbler outside the station who made a sound repair for fifteen rupees (£1=58 rupees). I sat on a chair and watched him and nearby fruit sellers with papayas and pineapples.

Eventually we were standing on the right platform awaiting the Rajasthan train along with hundreds of others. We were the only Europeans. More long distance trains were arriving as well as the stream of commuter trains. As each commuter train came into the station thousands poured out and an equal number pressed in with many hanging out of the doors. Amidst the general clamour I gradually became aware of singing coming from some of the crowded carriages. A young man told me that in these carriages there were groups singing bhagans or hymns. As their daily lives left little time for worship, they would sing bhagans or Hindu hymns on the train. And because this singing is popular, the carriages with singing groups are the most crowded. This seemed so Indian, so unbelievable. However, at a recent conference on India in Cambridge I told this story at a discussion group and an Indian said he had been part of a bhagan singing group on trains in Mumbai for several years and he has happy memories of this. Here is an example of how adaptable Hinduism is to the modern world.

RS

THE JOURNEY

Another day of adventure for the three of us. We had come to Mumbai just seven days ago yet already feel at home in Vile Parle, a suburb of this amazing city where extreme deprivation and great wealth live side by side. Our accommodation is basic but very clean and we are fortunate to have the luxury of comfortable beds, two showers and flushing toilets!

Three middle-aged English women travelling alone in this foreign country is a rare sight for the locals, but we are readily accepted into their friendly community and feel safe as we explore the many shops and market stalls. The area was affected by the recent monsoons and as a consequence the pavements and roads were desecrated leaving unbelievable destruction and mountains of rubbish with more dust than we could ever see in a lifetime on our streets back home. Yet through this terrible disruption, life happily continues. The sounds and smells of Mumbai is something that once experienced is never forgotten. The people of Vile Parle live in beautiful houses or, in staggering contrast, within corrugated tin shacks, on the roadside and in communities in the underpasses of the complex road systems. Parents send their young children to beg alongside the hundreds of cars and rickshaws in the hope of being given a few rupees to buy food. We have become accustomed to seeing very young children and their siblings sitting on the barriers of the dual carriageways amongst fast moving traffic just waiting for the next set of traffic lights to show 'stop' so they can come alongside us and attract our attention. We had been warned to avert our eyes from their pitiful faces but sat in an open rickshaw, it has been very difficult at times not to offer them something.

Close beside parked cars and within inches of the mayhem of moving vehicles, people walk in droves, their destination unknown. Hundreds of them, all day every day walking in either direction, but to where? Market traders, their stalls laden with colourful cloth, jewellery or fresh fruit and vegetables, set up their wares during late morning and continue to sell till past midnight. We had decided that that they probably sleep alongside their stalls, protective of their only means of livelihood. Besides, India never sleeps until it is ready, neither adult nor

child, for together they form the fabric of its very existence. Indeed, the aroma of the shops and market stalls together with that of spicy hot food, mingle with the smell of human sweat and Indian dust, till it settles permanently in our lungs. This is not commercialised India, but India in the raw, and we are privileged to be part of the experience.

Today, our chauffeur driven car arrived at 8.30 am to take us inland to Pune. The purpose of our visit was to meet three men associated with The Muktai Mission at Kedgaon to hand over money from a church in England which had generously supported the organisation. Pandita Ramabai, a recognised Indian Reformer apparently founded the mission in 1889 and as a widow herself, she was initially concerned with the welfare and education of widows. However, over the years its aims have expanded to support

मुंबई मुक्त कॉंग्रेस वालो आजाद मैदान एम.आर.सी.सी. सुनिल अहिरे

destitute women and children irrespective of their background and today set on a 100 acre plot their ministry includes education, medical care and homes for the elderly.

Interested to see and learn about this organisation for ourselves, we settled down in the comfort of our car ever thankful for the luxury of the airconditioning as the heat of the day became more intense. The first part of our journey took three and a half hours across breath-taking mountainous terrain and it seemed strange to stop at an isolated but modern service station for petrol and purchase welcome refreshments of a carton of orange juice and biscuit bar.

We had arranged to meet our hosts outside a church bookshop in central Pune and after the long journey, we welcomed the opportunity to stretch our legs. Together, we walked through the busy markets to a vegetarian restaurant where we enjoyed a much needed lunch. Our final destination for the night was about another hour inland, and now the last leg of the trip seemed to take forever in the searing heat of the afternoon.

On arrival at the mission, one of the men explained that he and his mother had been reunited here after forty years. As a little boy, she had left him in their care when she was widowed. She had returned to find her son, now a minister, working at the mission. Now elderly, blind and infirm she was being cared for in the mission nursing home, which stood in the hot, dusty grounds of the complex. He proudly introduced us to her in the room she shared with three other ladies and although their comforts were few, it was adequate. Most importantly, they felt loved, secure and cared for.

The room which had been allocated as our guest room for the night at the mission was sparse indeed. As we entered, its cold stone walls and floors sent a chill through our bones as we felt the presence of past inhabitants of this deeply religious community. An old wooden chest of drawers and mirror stood in the far corner. A green and pink floral curtain hung on a bamboo cane covering a window opening to the bathroom beyond. Just inside the front door was a wooden table on which stood a glass and a small bottle of water with a few plain biscuits in a sealed jam jar. Our room overlooked a grass quadrangle but the bars on the windows and above the solid wooden door stopped the failing daylight from entering.

We had been told to listen out for the gong which would sound the arrival of our evening meal in the mission dining room nearby. People come from all over the world to offer their help at the mission as we discovered whilst sharing a meagre meal of rice, mutton, vegetable dahl (like thick soup) and chapattis with an elderly American couple. Living a simple life on their farm south of New York they had made a promise to return to the mission every ten years. This year, to celebrate their fiftieth wedding anniversary they were accompanied by their two teenage grand-daughters who talked of their experience here with great enthusiasm. Sharing an evening prayer with this family and our hosts, we realised being at the mission was obviously a journey of faith for them all and we felt humbled by their loyalty and devotion.

Returning to our room for the evening we took turns to freshen up as best we could. The bathroom facilities were depressing. The words 'cattle shed' came to mind as I washed the dust from my feet with cold water from the tap and used the, thankfully flushing, but grimy, toilet.

Our beds resembled wooden tables covered in the thinnest of mattresses with a thin blanket, sheet and pillow that had long since seen better days. A grubby blue quilt, folded at the end of each bed, would be reluctantly used during the night, for unlike Mumbai which remained humid, the temperature dropped dramatically here. Then, reflecting on the day's journey, we three middle-aged English women tried to settle down for the night, resolving never to take our lives for granted again.

JC

LOOKING AT THE MOON

The man in the moon, his face shining bright,
Bathing the world below with subtle light;
Wondering who his next visitor will be,
Will their arrival fill him with sadness or glee?
For over the years man has his solitude disturbed
But sadly no complaints from him are ever heard.
Rockets and shuttles the super-powers have sent into space
Trying to be first to establish colonies upon his face.
Friendship now the super-powers try to seek,
So why bother disturbing that smile, looking so meek?
Should we not leave the man in the moon in peace to rest?
For on earth there are more pressing issues to contest.
While half the world to bed still hungry goes,
Rockets are launched searching for life of
which no-one knows.
If one day man all his problems on earth can surpass,
No-one should object to him flying off to explore that
heavenly mass.

GB

THE ARTIST

What does she think?
What does she see?
Attacking brush in hand, the virgin canvas.

Oils, pastels,
mediums solely to express and bring thoughts to life.

Hours fade,
no food, drinks pass her lips,
Completion before sustenance.

Competitions.
Exhibitions.
Notoriety.

RJ

WINTER WALK

Wind cuts the face and pulls at hair.
Fields spread before me,
Vistas of green.
Distant hedgerows cut the land.

Puddles sparkle along tyre tracks.
Stark trees, shadow against the grey sky.
Crows thrown on the wind,
like black rags.

Birds on cables ruffle against the cold air,
Shake their heads and stretch legs.
A pheasant stalks.
Its red cheeks vibrate against green shoots.

Wellington boots part the mud that pulls against the pace.
Hands thrust into pockets.
The red barn rises ahead,
a taste of rain in the air.

Inside, damp and quiet,
Gloom lit by the open door.
Leaves scurry past.
Darkness falls.

BH

NO GETTING COLD FEET

It's no good getting cold feet
When life's adversities you have to meet.
Troubles come and troubles go
But life goes on, don't you know.

It's no good getting cold feet
When a partner you want to meet,
Faint hearts never won maidens fair,
So push ahead, don't dally there.

It's no good getting cold feet
When the opposition turns up the heat.
In a debate speak loud and clear
To show them they've much to fear.

It's no good getting cold feet
When you've got a handicap to beat.
Focus on what you've got to do
And you'll become a winner too.

It's no good getting cold feet
If your exam work is far from neat.
Concentrate on what you know
And your tidiness will start to grow.

It's no good getting cold feet
Or like a lost lamb start to bleat.
When a problem clouds your mind,
The solution's there for you to find.

GB

MY 'LUCKY DAY'

My friend Joan and I had been on a late lunchtime break, i.e. from one until two o'clock. It was wartime so obviously the food wouldn't be luxurious - far from it; a buttered bun and a cup of weak tea at a local cafe was all we had that day. Sometimes my Mum would make me a few sandwiches but that wasn't too often because, with rationing, she had enough to think about in order to get main meals on the table.

I had settled down at the typewriter to transcribe my shorthand notes, while my boss and his secretary-cum-P.A. were in his office making arrangements to visit one of the firm's shops, in view of the fact that he was in charge of Branch Maintenance in the absence of the Estate Manager, who had been called up for National Service. The time would have been around 2.15 p.m.

I heard nothing. The first recollection I had was of seeing the pint bottle of blue-black ink on the window sill with one-third of its contents missing. The top part of the bottle was nowhere to be seen and the remaining ink was trickling down the wall underneath the sill.

Then I noticed that the blinds had disappeared from the windows; they had been ripped from their fittings and flung against the wall opposite by the blast. And my filing baskets were missing also.

I noticed the back of my right hand was bleeding; the cut wasn't serious but glass had cut into a vein. I remember thinking I had best go and wash the wound in the Ladies washroom, which I did and then wrapped my handkerchief round the cut as tightly as I could with only one hand, and returned to my office.

As I was leaving the washroom I saw a young man

coming down the corridor towards me from an office at the far end of the building; he was bleeding profusely from a deep gash right across his nose. He was, in fact, an auditor who was going through the firm's books, so I didn't know him at all. I wasn't quite sure what to do, being only seventeen at the time, but I took him into the Gents washroom and pulled down the roller towel, giving it to him with the instructions to apply 'digital compression' to his nose. That was about all I could think of at the time; my knowledge of first aid wasn't all that extensive.

Then I went back to my office to find out how my boss and his secretary had fared. They were both in a state of shock. Poor man, my boss was in his seventies and was only still working because the younger men had been called up. I told him what I had done with the auditor and although he was very shaken-up (but not injured, thankfully) he proceeded to do what he could for the injured chap.

It transpired that both of my colleague had heard the slight 'whoosh' of the V2 as it came down and had taken cover - my boss had put his head under his desk, while Mrs. C. had sheltered behind one of the filing cabinets.

Apparently no air raid siren had sounded so no-one had any warning of the impending raid; this was quite normal. However, when a VI raid was imminent the public usually got prior warning and could take shelter. But with the V2s there was no warning and therefore no way of knowing when they would arrive.

On returning to my office I found the floor strewn with debris. All the doors were off their hinges - and they were of the very heavy, self-closing type - but the blast had torn them from their fittings: and there was no glass left in the window frames.

Our Works Office and the Factory had also sustained a

lot of damage, the latter especially because it had a glass roof. Many people were injured, some killed, and everyone was suffering from shock and moving around aimlessly. I managed to get through on the internal phone system to the Typists' Pool, to enquire how my friend Joan was; luckily she was unhurt and had been told to get off home.

The commissionnaire at the entrance to our Head Office was a friend of the family so I went to find out how he was. He had a nasty cut on the top of his head, so we decided to seek treatment at the local First Aid Station. On arrival we could see that it would be useless to wait for our injuries to be seen to there. The queue was very long with people suffering from cuts - many of which had been caused by flying glass - so the majority of victims were bleeding, mostly from arms, legs and heads. Whilst we were deciding what to do next, several badly injured people were carried past the queue to get immediate treatment because, in spite of tourniquets, they were still losing a lot of blood.

So we decided to hop on a bus and get to the First Aid Centre nearest to our homes. I remember the conductor would not let us pay any fare! Of course, he knew what had happened and, like everyone else in similar circumstances, was very sympathetic.

On arrival at the First Aid Centre we had to give our name and address, then go in to see the duty doctor. He turned out to be a very elderly man and, despite several attempts, had found it very difficult to get the anti-tetanus injection into my arm. After the doctor had inserted a few stitches, the nurse dressed the wound, painted it with some yellow stuff (which I presume was some sort of antiseptic) and put my arm in a sling. It was at this point that I discovered I had a cut on the right hand side of my face as well; this did not need stitching but was given a liberal coating of the yellow stuff.

Imagine the look on my Mum's face when she opened the door to me on my arrival home. With a partially painted face and one arm in a sling, she was naturally shocked. She had already been called out to attend the incident which I had just left, as she was a member of the W.V.S. These ladies worked in teams of six to provide hot drinks and food to the Air Raid Wardens and Firemen when they were working on a bomb site. Naturally she didn't want to leave me but I insisted that she must go because otherwise the team would be one member short. I remember telling her that I did know how to treat shock – a drink of hot, sweet tea was the answer. So eventually she went off to do her duty.

Some time later a friend of mine called in to see if I was all right. Whilst on the train coming home from the City she had seen smoke rising from the direction of my firm and was concerned to know that I was safe. During her visit I decided to comb the glass fragments out of my hair and it was then that I noticed the weals on my legs and arms. They looked as if I'd been slashed by a leather thong. It was at this point that my friend voiced her concern, telling me that my face was swelling rapidly and she was going to call the doctor - he lived just across the road. This she did, but before he came I had fainted. The two of them managed to get me onto my bed – and that was the last I can remember of the day.

I was unconscious from that Tuesday afternoon until the following Friday morning. The doctor thought maybe I was going down with pneumonia, or perhaps it was just shock. He personally thought it may have been the anti-tetanus serum which did not agree with me; he had heard of several cases where people had reacted badly to the injection. On the other hand, there was a possibility that the needle itself had infected me with something or other.

Whatever, I came to with my Mum combing my hair, making a parting and putting a slide in it, just as if I was still a child at school. But I was a teenager, used to wearing my hair in large sweeps!

I was off work for almost three weeks and went to relatives in the country to recuperate. Everyone was very sympathetic and many wanted to know what had happened. I was an object of much curiosity.

When I returned to the office I discovered that dozens of splinters of glass had passed me and lodged in the wooden filing cabinets on the other side of the room. Workmen were employed to dig out all the little shards and put a fresh surface on the cabinets.

Weeks later I was interviewed concerning my injuries; I remember the doctor who interviewed me smoked Du Maurier cigarettes. During a later session, with a different person, I was awarded five guineas for the pain of my injuries and 2s.6d. for new stockings, plus three clothing coupons for the latter.

I often wonder how so much shattered glass managed to miss me on that afternoon, when the V2 killed and wounded so many people.

I feel it really must have been my LUCKY DAY!

DM

MINUS 22

It's Saturday morning halfpast ten
I'm counting frozen chickens again

It's part of my job that's what I do
Counting frozen chickens at minus twenty-two.

I don't just count chickens there are other products too,
In my freezer Saturday mornings at minus twenty two.

My freezer is forty feet long twelve feet wide
with an amazing array of products inside.
Nuggets and chips, plain chickens too
Neatly stacked in my freezer at minus twenty two.

RJ

METAL 'DETECTRISTS'

Figures in a ploughed field,
Scanning.
Listening for treasure or old coke can
Appendages swinging
Treading with kid gloves,
Some archeologically insouciant.

RJ

IT'S SO BRACING

Sardine packed tourists promenading
with kiss-me-quick smiles,
pass Kelly's eye and hungry bandits in neon facades.
While
Fast food packaging feels at home in the road
like Saturday night boy racers cruising round town.

Mighty pier long lost to the sea,
a landmark for pensive donkeys plying
their trade in the sand.
Where
Planning permission evaded castles grow,
then die like lovers footprints in the ebb and the flow.

Sticky faced hands from rock in innumerable disguises,
merge with candy flossed hands and fish and chip eaters.
Hearing,
Funfair emotions pervading all-seeing clock tower,
and the jolly fisherman,
that finds it all so bracing.

RJ

HOW'S YOUR MEMORY?

For example, can you remember what you were doing on the day Queen Elizabeth II was crowned? I am a Londoner - in fact, because I was born within the sound of Bow Bells, I am a true Cockney. In view of this it is not surprising that when I grew up I lived and worked in the metropolis.

During the weeks leading up to the Coronation, business concerns in the London area were invited to request tickets to view the Procession from one of the many Stands which were to be erected. I was working in an office in Bedford Square (which is just off Tottenham Court Road) and when our tickets were received a ballot was held of all interested parties. I think the organisation for which I worked was allocated about 20 places in one of the Stands, several of which had been set up alongside the London Parks.

But, just thirty minutes before we left the office on the day prior to the Coronation, a messenger arrived with two of the tickets that had been allocated to us. It appeared the person who had been lucky enough to win these tickets had just received a request urging him to travel immediately to Scotland, as a relative had met with an accident and was not expected to live more than a few hours. So he was going to fly up to Scotland at the earliest possible time and had decided to return his tickets by personal messenger so that someone else could use them.

In view of the fact that it really was too late to contact any of the other interested people (who were, in the main, company directors) it was decided that the two returned tickets should be offered to staff members, in order of precedence. I was fortunate to be offered a ticket because neither of the two secretaries who were senior to me wished to attend; but a colleague in my own office was lucky and secured a ticket.

If my memory serves me correctly the tickets cost £4 each. Needless to say, we didn't get any sleep that night! It was agreed that my colleague should go home to get some warm clothing, that her Dad would drop her round to my home and my husband would ensure that we got to the Tube station safely. We had to be in our places by 6.30 a.m., and special early trains were laid on throughout the night.

Our particular tickets were for places in a Stand bordering Green Park, and on leaving the station we had to find our places - which was no easy task. The seating was very basic, the weather was cold and damp, and we were glad to have made good provision for the hours we were to spend in the Stand, i.e. waterproofs, blankets and vacuum flasks of hot drink. We were grateful too for the primitive toilet facilities which were available.

Waiting for the event seemed endless. We watched as the policemen guarding the route changed shifts; and the roadsweepers got enthusiastic cheers whenever they came along to clean up after the horses. And, needless to say, there was plenty of cheerful banter between the spectators.

My recollections of the actual procession are very scant. I remember it rained on and off and we all got wet and felt cold despite having blankets with us. The horses and carriages were all resplendent and colourful; the bands very loud as they passed by, and the marching absolutely in time.

The Queen, of course, looked radiant and happy; she really did look very pretty. And Mr. Churchill stood up and waved to the crowd as he passed our Stand. I did take a few photographs but the light was very poor on the day.

Once the Procession had commenced it seemed to pass very quickly.

We were very tired after the uncomfortable journey home, with so many people all leaving the area at the same time.

Actually, my best memory of that part of June is not the Coronation but the fact that I found I was pregnant with my first baby!

DM

FREEDOM 2008

Somewhere on London streets
A broken butterfly lies.
Forged by blood in distant Chinese slum,
it's crafted like a garnet leaf
fluttering briefly on a shoulder;
but tangling with silken scarf from Taiwan,
flies unhinged into foreign confusion.

Mai Lei, student of Art, finds it,
strokes its bright wings
tenderly.
I will bring it – she thinks –
to my half-blind grandmother, Ching,
Daughter of the Revolution,
to remind her of that flight.

JS

CONFUSION

Alison carried the mugs of coffee to the table; as she put them down she noticed her hands shaking.

"Look, Dave, you can't treat me like a little girl. I'm twenty-four not fourteen. My hen night is my time not yours and you can't tell me how to enjoy myself or how to drink."

Dave looked up at her. "I want you to enjoy it, but there's no need to get wrecked and carried home is there."

He looked like a hurt schoolchild again. They had been going out together for four years and he had only popped the question three months ago. He could be so frustrating with his slow steady ways and his attention to detail. He had planned the wedding like a military operation, everyone involved knew their duties. She didn't know why he had bothered with a best man at all.

"I've already given in and arranged the hen night for the weekend before the wedding. I'm stuck in an Estate Agents office five days a week, I need to breathe and get out. Just because you enjoy living like a hermit it doesn't mean I have to."

Dave stood up and began pacing. "I'm sorry, I don't want to restrict your life, it's just that I worry about you. Sometimes I don't even know why you're marrying me."

She watched him walk back and forth and felt suddenly sorry for him. She hadn't told him but she was worried about the commitment she had made. They were opposites, but didn't opposites attract? She knew as well that her mother and father would be devastated if the wedding didn't go through, they thought Dave was just the man for her. A calming influence with a steady job in accountancy, what could be better?

"I'm sorry too," she said, "It's probably just stress; let's just forget about it and start again."

She walked over to him and kissed him. He breathed a sigh, held her tight and kissed her softly, "I love you so much."

Alison felt tears welling up as she replied, "I love you too, darling, and don't worry about me, Angie will get me home. It's you I'm worried about, you know, an old man of twenty-seven going on the razzle with his mates."

Dave laughed. "Two pints is about my limit these days, any more and I get a terrible hangover."

It was Friday night and she had just finished getting dressed when the doorbell rang and Angie walked in.

"God, talk about dressed to kill," she said, producing a bottle of vodka.

"You don't look too bad yourself. Don't forget I'm the star tonight."

Angie laughed, "I don't think any of the girls will outshine you."

The evening went well – the women had made their presence known in three bars and were looking forward to hitting the nightclubs. Alison, now sporting a plastic tiara and wedding veil and covered in streamers, felt agreeably drunk. She visited the loo and when she looked in the mirror her eyes sparkled with life; she felt free and wild and grinned back at herself.

Returning to the table she joined her raucous band of girlfriends. One of the young women had produced a selection of sex toys from a carrier bag and screams of laughter erupted as plastic shapes buzzed their way across the table unaided.

"Genuine Anne Summers these, half-price to you Alison," Lisa said. "I think I prefer the real thing," Alison replied, to more screams of laughter.

She had just finished her drink when a man approached the table carrying a multicoloured cocktail complete with sparklers.

"For the bride-to-be," he said.

She looked into his face and was struck as if by a blow. He was gorgeous, his blue eyes pierced her soul, his lips were firm and kissable, his smile seemed to just melt her heart.

"Oh, thank you," she said, staring back into those bottomless eyes. "Alan," he said, holding out his hand.

She took his hand to a chorus of, "Oohs," from the girls who immediately grabbed a chair from another table for him. Alison found herself gazing at him again, dressed in a shirt and trousers, his dark hair trimmed perfectly and stubble-darkened face. He looked at her and there was a connection she was sure of it. It was as though a telepathic message penetrated her mind. "I want you," he was saying. She licked her lips – they felt dry, but she knew also that she was giving him a message.

What the hell am I doing! she said to herself, breaking the spell. You're getting married to a man you love, what are you doing. She looked away but could somehow feel those eyes looking into her mind itself.

She heard some movement and saw Alan who had been entertaining the others, had moved his chair next to hers.

"You haven't finished your cocktail," he said, "can I get you something else?"

She felt angry. Who the hell did he think he was, walking into her life now and setting her body alight. It must be the drink, yes that's it, she was drunk, but somehow she didn't believe it.

"No, thank you, we are just leaving, aren't we girls."

They looked back vacantly and she stared at them and raised her eyebrows in earnest.

Angie was first to move. "Come on, girls, more booze and men ahead."

Alison turned to Alan hoping to avoid his gaze and said, "Thank you for the drink."

"No problem," he said (that smile beaming again), "I hope the wedding goes well."

Once they got outside Angie grabbed her arm and said, "Another time, eh, I think you pulled there."

"Christ, Angie, grow up," she said.

The rest of the night went slowly, her thoughts returning to Alan. She wondered why she felt so struck by a stranger whom she had hardly spoken to. There was also guilt – Dave was such a good man, a solid man, she loved him, didn't she?

The next morning she woke late, and gazed at the ceiling through a painful fog of a hangover. After half an hour she found herself sitting cross-legged on the bed. Snatches of the previous night edged their way into her throbbing brain. Then there was a sudden rush of guilt that kicked her stomach. That man, Alan, yes Alan. What was that all about, she laughed to herself. I mean he was handsome and everything but what was she doing cracking up like that.

As she made coffee his name kept coming back to her. The more her head cleared the more she remembered those eyes and that easy smile that invited her in. She felt confused and her anger boiled. You can't do this, what about Dave? You can't just dump a man you've known for four years, shared a bed with, loved, and accepted a marriage proposal from, for some bloke in a pub.

But she felt it wasn't just lust that had attracted her to Alan, there was something else – a fear of getting trapped into a marriage. Of being expected to be a nice housewife in a nice house. She had to meet him again, she would see whether it was just a drunken attraction or if her feelings were real. She had to know, before it was too late.

She met Angie outside the pub at seven thirty. It was early, but she didn't want to chance missing him.

"Here you are,"Angie said, "I'm only going to say what I said on the phone, I think you're mad. You've got your whole future set up and you want to throw it away on some flash bloke you don't even know."

"I don't want to throw it all away, but wouldn't you want to know the truth before it was too late? What if he is the one and I'm signing my life away?" Alison said.

"What about Dave? He loves you, what about your family?" Angie said.

"I do love Dave, but what I felt last night was more than love. It was a true connection with a man and I can't help my feelings. He may not turn up and that's that, but I just want to know."

"He was stunning though, wasn't he? Tell you the truth I was thinking of coming back here tonight on my own and poaching him," Angie laughed.

"Cow," Alison replied.

They sat at a table with a good view of the door and bar. Alison looking up eagerly every time the door opened.

"Steady woman, don't look so keen or some other bloke will try it on," Angie said.

The pub filled and the noise got louder until conversation was by shouting. She normally loved this atmosphere but this was painful, it was now half past nine and still no sign of Alan. Then she saw him walking in, he must have come in through the back door. She kicked Angie under the table. "Ow, what is it," she shouted back.

Alison pointed at the bar. He was dressed in a casual shirt again and seemed taller than she remembered. Then to her dismay a woman joined him, they chatted and he kissed her.

"Come on, let's go," she said.

"No wait, look," Angie said.

She looked back and saw another man join them. He kissed the young woman and led her by the arm to the window, Alan followed with a tray of drinks.

"What now?" Angie said.

"I don't know, we wait I suppose."

She stared at the little group, they all chatted and laughed, the men stood either side of the woman, she couldn't bear it. Then Alan looked around the room, his gaze stopped at their table and he took the drink from his mouth and smiled and waved. Alison waved back, perhaps too enthusiastically.

He spoke to the others and made his way to the table.

"Well, if it isn't the bride-to-be and her lovely assistant, can I get you a drink?" he said, smiling.

Alison looked into his face and it was there again, that feeling of helplessness. She just wanted him to take her in his arms and take her away from this muddle of a life.

"What about your friends?" she asked.

"That's my sister, Sam and her latest. I'm glad to get away to be honest, playing gooseberry doesn't suit me."

He went to the bar waving at his sister and pointing to Alison's table. For a minute she thought they would join them, but they didn't move. She did not want anyone interfering tonight.

"What do you want me to do?" Angie said, "I don't like playing gooseberry either."

"Just stay for your drink. If it's going well make your excuses and go. I have to know, Angie," she said.

"The way you've turned to jelly, you do know,"she replied, smiling.

Alan returned to the table and sat next to Alison. For the next half hour he spoke only to her.

The more he spoke the more sure she became.

"Well, I think it's past my bedtime," Angie said, getting up. "Oh, leaving so soon,"Alan said, standing up and shaking her hand. As she left, Angie turned and raised her mobile at Alison. She smiled and nodded back.

"Well what do you want to do now? We can move on or my flat is around the comer if you fancy wine and some quieter music," he shouted. This was it then, she thought. It was obvious what was on Alan's mind but what did she feel?

"Well, it is noisy in here, let's take the wine and soft music choice,"she said.

She knew what she had said, but she couldn't believe she had said it. She was offering herself on a plate to him. This time there was no excuse, this was cold and calculating.

They walked laughing together for about ten minutes until they reached the flat. Once inside it felt warm and she didn't know why but she felt safe and at home.

Alan poured the wine and as promised soft music flooded the room. They sat facing each other on the sofa.

"Are you sure you want to be here? You're almost a married woman you know," he said, sipping his wine.

Alison stared back into those dark-blue pits. It wasn't possible but she thought she could feel her own pupils dilating.

"I haven't done anything yet,"she said.

"Well, if you feel like I do we can soon change that," he said, leaning forward and kissing her gently on the lips.

She felt her heart race. If she did this there was no going back. She hesitated then put her arms around his neck and kissed him, closing her eyes and letting him flow over her.

The following morning she awoke in Alan's bed. She could hear the shower running and she smiled to herself. She still wasn't sure if it was love or lust. But she did know one thing, she felt happy and free. Even if it did not work out between her and Alan, she knew it was over between her and Dave. She picked up her mobile. "Angie?" she said...

BH

BLOSSOM AND DECAY

As I drew back the curtains one January day
I marvelled at the picture I saw:
Silhouetted against the cobalt blue sky -
A Bride, on her Wedding Day?

Snow covered her shapely figure
resembling a white velvet gown;
While satin ribbons and clusters of pearls
replaced frozen pathways and streams.

As the sun peeped over the horizon
its rays caught the uppermost point
And for just a fleeting moment
a diamante head-dress appeared
Above the frozen crags
which depicted her shoulder-length hair.

Rousing myself from this day-dream ...
a beautiful start to the day
I decided the mountain could only be female
to appear in such a wonderful way.

And as I continued to lovingly gaze
I exclaimed my appreciation;
She really had reached heights of perfection
to blossom on her Wedding Day.

Later on in the day, whilst walking the dogs,
I encountered a small village pond
Which, due to the freezing weather,
was shrouded in a covering of snow.

Surrounded by various hedges
and several species of trees,
Because of a ferocious winter wind
they had lately shed all of their leaves.

So, now they stood both stark and bare
cloaked only in rime and hoar frost
Resembling magnificent statues
displayed in a garden of peace.

The scene was breathtakingly beautiful;
the silence so tranquil too
That I was moved to imagine
the picture depicted life's end.

DM

DAISIES

Wait until night then
spread your star-white, light-yellow-hearts
through the jade.
Spade cannot dim you
blade will only trim you.
Raise your heads
above the parapet,
invade the lawn
and smile
in glee!

JS

A ROYAL VISITOR

Tom Chambers switched on his television. It was five-fifteen time for his favourite programme "The Weakest Link." It wasn't that Tom cared much for Anne Robinson. He watched the programme because the questions asked kept his brain active.

Living alone in his cottage a short distance from the village Tom didn't get many visitors. He found calling out the answers relieved his boredom and loneliness.

He had thought about drawing the curtains but decided against doing so till after the show had ended by which time it would be dark.

No sooner had he sat down when a squeak from his garden gate drew his attention. His garden gate served two purposes; firstly it kept the local farmer's sheep out of his garden when they were driven up the lane from field to field. It also acted as a doorbell with its squeaky hinges announcing the arrival of any visitors the moment they attempted to open it. Ben the postman kept threatening to bring some oil for the hinges that made its opening hard work.

Tom rose, walked over to the window and took a quick look out. Seeing no one there he re-seated himself in front of the television disgusted at contestants who had failed to bank any money in the first round.

While they were voting off 'the weakest link' his security light came on. Rising once more he peered out the window. Failing to see anyone or anything moving in the overgrown jungle he called his garden he sat down once again to concentrate on the show.

It was only a matter of minutes before the light came on again.

Hobbling over to the window he still couldn't see any cause for it to come on. Starting to feel a little concerned Tom drew the curtains shutting out its glare. Glancing at the television he saw the contestants were having as bad a night as he was, only managing to bank four hundred and fifty pounds in four rounds. This was fuel for Miss Robinson's sarcastic wit and wasn't she making the most of it!

"I'd show them how to go on if I entered," he said to himself as disgusted by their efforts he went in the kitchen to prepare an early tea.

No sooner had he started buttering the bread when a loud bang on the front door forced him to retrace his steps. Cautiously he opened the door. "How nice it is to see you again, your highness," he proclaimed upon seeing who his visitor was. "You'd better come in and sit down while I get you a drink then I must ring the palace to let them know where you are," he said leading his visitor inside.

His visitor walked over and stood in front of Tom's open fire. "You'll scorch if you stand there too long," Tom warned him. Heeding Tom's words he backed away from the fire a little before lying down on the hearth rug. Tom breathed a sigh of relief for he wouldn't have been very popular if the King had burnt his only coat.

Going into the kitchen he took a pint of milk from the fridge and returned to stand it in the hearth. "It'll soon take the chill off it. I know you don't like your drinks too cold as they play havoc with your highness's old teeth," he said joining his guest upon the rug.

Five minutes later he rose; after testing the temperature of the bottle, he carried it into the kitchen emerging moments later with its contents in a large bowl. "Is it to your taste?" he asked his guest, who rolled his eyes as he lapped the bowl dry. "I take it that's a yes then," he said as guest, thirst quenched, stretched out again to enjoy the fire's warmth. Reaching out Tom grasped the limb his visitor held out for him to stroke. Within seconds it fell away, his guest deep asleep.

Quietly he moved away, the heavy breathing telling him his guest would not be moving far for sometime. He picked up the telephone and dialled a familiar number.

"Who is it?" A startled voice came down the line.

"Sebastian, it's me, Tom. Have you not noticed that his majesty has gone walkabout again?" Tom waited. He could hear Sebastian moving, a door being opened and then him shouting, "Dario where are you?" before returning to the phone. "That silly old fool Dario was supposed to be keeping an eye on him but I bet the vodka's taken priority over that," he said.

Sebastian Jones owned what remained of a once successful circus. Its caravans and trailers were now quartered in the old railway yard a mile or so from Tom's cottage. Almost all the animals having been either sold off or died from old age, Dario was the only other person living on the site. Sebastian couldn't afford to employ him but they had an agreement; in exchange for staying in his caravan Dario helped look after the few remaining animals and tried to keep the site tidy.

"Has his highness come visiting you again?" Sebastian asked sensing that was what Tom was ringing about.

"Yes, he's here fast asleep in front of the fire," Tom replied.

"When I find Dario we'll come and collect him. You know how awkward he can be if Dario's not there," Sebastian said before ringing off.

Twenty minutes later Tom's security light came on. Looking down the garden he saw Sebastian and Dario approaching the house. What an odd couple they made, Sebastian, wearing jeans and a waxed jacket while Dario, who was rather short, wore his red ring-master coat with his black hat tilted to one side.

"Is the old gentleman ready to be taken home yet?" asked Dario.

"I think so," Tom replied leading the pair of them through to his front-room. Cautiously Dario knelt beside the sleeping body and slipped a collar and chain around its neck. "Wake-up, your highness, it's time to go home," he said stroking its long flowing mane.

Leo opened his eyes and rose to his feet. Tom let him lick his fingers before he walked off after Dario. Sebastian, firmly grasping the chain, thanked Tom once again for taking care of his old friend then followed close behind.

Watching them load Leo into their van Tom felt sorry for The King of Jungle but was glad the lion had friends like Sebastian and Dario to care for him in his old age. He wondered how long he would have to wait before his royal visitor graced him with his presence again.

GB

PRIMITIVE

Khaki-coloured eyes, they were
hooded, never blinking.
They mesmerised the terrified
who guessed their evil thinking.
They saw the world with ancient sight,
they glistened in the semi-light,
they penetrated pitch at night -
the hunter slowly slinking.

JS

SENSES OR SENSATIONS

Touching a sumptuous velvet cushion –
or silky lingerie.
Know the warmth of woollen mittens
or a cup of hot sweet tea.
Stroking a fluffy kitten or
patting a sturdy dog.
Have a pillow filled with feathers;
watch the glow of a burning log.

See mountains in the distance
and the differing shades of fields.
Trees in bud, and then in leaf,
the colour each one yields.
A sunlit pond bordered by flags
and shrubs of every hue;
Morning dew on grass and bushes
against a sky of blue.

Congratulations on a job well done;
a welcoming hug or kiss.
Stepping out of fashionable shoes
can sometimes be sheer bliss!
Travelling abroad to explore new lands,
to try out foreign food.
Feeling the warmth of sun on your skin
is sure to improve your mood.

The smell of sizzling sausages,
of apple pie, or cake.
A Sunday roast, hot new bread,
or a hock of gammon steak.

The taste of favourite foods
be it pudding, pie or tart:
From simple toast and marmalade
to wedding cakes rivalling art.

Small children playing in the park
or splashing in the sea
While their grandparents snooze on a sunny bench
or sip a cup of tea.
What a thrill when a daughter tells you
she's soon to become a bride,
Or your son, in his excitement to be a Dad,
chooses in you to confide.

So while we all would like the ability
to use our main five treasures,
Some are dulled by age or illness,
others never know such pleasures.
Sensations are usually triggered by senses but
its difficult to define.
So, let's forget the facts and logic
no enjoyment undermine.

DM

VIRTUAL BEEKEEPING

I read it on the web, www virtual beekeeping dot com.
Virtual beekeeping - I was intrigued so I scrolled down.
The site explained; watch your very own hive or hives from
the comfort of your own home, no equipment to purchase,
no mess to worry about, but most important no stings, and
you will receive a honey crop at the year end. Invest today!

That's for me, I thought. Never been a country bumpkin,
rural studies and all that, so I e-mailed the beekeeper. He
replied by suggesting that I take a short course at my local
college so that I would have some knowledge about the life
of the honey bee and I would understand the terminology
of the different parts of the hive during manipulation of
my bees.

I enrolled for the one-evening-per-week-six-week-course.
I learnt about workers, drones, supers, crown boards, brood
chambers and much, much more. But most important of
all the beekeeper must find his queen bee.

There were twelve of us on the course. I was the only
member that didn't have a beekeeping suit or smoker (the
smoker is used to calm the bees). No need, I told them and
explained why.

Armed with certificate in hand, I e-mailed my beekeeper
who returned my communication saying that he would
take me to my bees on Saturday, weather permitting. I
know honeybees don't like being disturbed during
inclement weather, learnt that on the course as well.

Saturday came - I switched on my computer. "I'm going
to your bees," came the message. "You can watch via my
web cam."

Just off the A15 is a minor road (one of many I hasten to
add) and the English countryside is a picture in late Spring

and early Summer, trees in leaf, masses of blossom gives you that "glad to be alive" feeling. I watched him open the five-barred gate that put a temporary halt to our journey and then saw pheasant and partridge scatter as he drove parallel to a small copse, home to his apiary.

The web cam went blank during disconnection from the dash and attachment to his bee suit hood. He walked into the wood and I saw his/our apiary. Six hives in total arranged in a neat little row. One was mine and I wondered how many other people were watching waiting to see into their hive/hives.

Mine was number five so I had to be patient while he manipulated the first four. He spoke continually as he worked, stressing at each hive he opened that he must find the queen. Without her the colony is in turmoil.

I/we watched our bees working as he removed and inspected each comb, turning them and checking both sides and then replacing them in their original position in the brood chamber. He reiterated the importance of finding the queen in mine and all preceding hives.

After removing the outer comb in one brood chamber he began to search for eggs; this told him that the queen was "in lay", tiny eggs 3mm long standing vertical in the comb, one to each cell. Some lay horizontal, others resembling a tiny letter 'c.'

The beekeeper held the comb so that I and all the other hive holders could see her. He then replaced the comb along with its queen very carefully back into the brood chamber, and then systematically checked the remainder of the combs. The bees were becoming agitated; the weather was cooling, so he closed the hive to prevent the brood becoming chilled.

He apologised for not telling me or the other hive holders

about the quantity of honey in each super (that's the box on top of each brood chamber where the bees store any surplus honey) and told us that we would receive a crop but he did not want to commit himself as to how much and he hoped it would reflect well on our investment.

Months passed; we e-mailed daily as I had so many questions to ask each time we saw our bees on our computer screens. All busy, bringing in lots of pollen. We could even tell which flowers they were working by the colour of the pollen on their legs.

I had begun to feel a sense of disappointment at not having my own hive of bees; I now wanted to see the bees close up not via a computer screen. Something was missing but I didn't know what it was, so I bought myself a beehive and put it in my garden, no bees I hasten to add. I told myself, no equipment, no mess, no stings, who wants to keep bees?

A few wild honeybees inspected the empty hive - I watched them going in from the comfort of my shed, then dashed outside to see them come out. Not one took up residence.... I felt relieved with just a tinge of sadness.

I did an even more stupid thing the other day - bought myself a beekeeping suit! Not going to wear it though, or maybe I shall, just to stand and watch the bees going in and out of my hive.

I checked my e-mail; "I'm going to spin off your honey today. I shall mount the web cam in my honey house and you can watch the results of your bees' efforts."

He set up his equipment and we watched as the honey poured out of the extractor through a wire mesh and into a settling tank. The honey is left here overnight and this allows any extraneous matter, bits of wax, etc to float to the top. The honey is then jarred and labelled.

He was vigilant, ensuring we all received our rightful share. Mine was 60 x lb jars. I was pleased and we still had our bees for next year; not a bad return on our investment. I could sell some of my honey and buy equipment, bees - no, don't be stupid, no bees, no mess, no stings.

He e-mailed me later that day, "I shall bring the honey on Saturday." (We had agreed that we should have only one delivery per year to avoid unnecessary travelling costs.) "We can talk then." Talk, talk I thought, what does he want to talk about? I bet he wants more money for next year. Men are all the same - greedy!

The door bell rang - I had prepared myself for a fight. I opened the door but before I had a chance to say anything, "I've come looking for my Queen."

"Pardon, what did you say?"

"I've come looking for my queen and at last I've met her and I want to be your drone...."

RJ

'UNTITLED'

How do I portray my love in ink,
Showing I need you like meat needs salt?*
And how do I keep your love,
Never abuse the trust you place with me?

But what is love?
A look,
Touch,
A smile that says I'm always here –
Or is it simply a need for togetherness?

RJ

* Story from Arabian Nights

FOOD FOR THOUGHT

Recently a friend invited me to visit somewhere I had never been before, so I readily agreed to accompany her. The venue was a very specialist establishment .... it produced statues in Ice. I was intrigued, wondering how on earth so many different and diverse items could be produced from ice.

On arriving, the first thing I saw was a sculptured elephant - a gorgeous creature with its trunk raised – then there was a perfect giraffe and also a polar bear, all in glistening white form. There was a display of rampant lions - such heroic creatures, a unicorn - obviously created by someone with a vivid imagination but just as majestic as I would envisage it to be.

Towards the centre of the workshop was a display of human figures, both male and female, beautifully detailed and lifesize, some naked and others clothed. Close by was a group of cherubs in various positions and carrying either flowers or instruments.

Smaller creatures were also on display. Squirrels, rabbits, foxes and really beautiful deer of different sizes. I was amazed at their intricate detail and envious of the expertise of the sculptor – they took such pride in their efforts to attain perfection.

Another section contained scenery of mountainous terrain, the items were breathtakingly beautiful and so cleverly depicted in glistening white ice. All in all my visit turned out to be a revelation and I was so pleased I had accepted my friend's invitation to accompany her.

I was told that most of the items were due to be transported to various venues within the next twenty-four hours, to be displayed at imminent events, and that after a few hours they would slowly melt and disappear. This news saddened me because such a lot of thought and work had gone into the formation of these wonderful creations - and they really were very beautiful. No doubt the purchasers would be delighted to receive them and obviously realised the statues would not be long-lived. They would go on display, give a lot of pleasure to many people over a short space of time, and that was sufficient incentive to procure them.

Imagine my dismay when, a few days after my visit, I read in a national newspaper that, due to an electricity cut during the night-time hours, all the statues I had viewed a few days previously had been destroyed, melting in the workshop because the emergency supply had failed to take over from the failed mains current.

Such beautiful works of art now reduced to water;

I felt very sad, for myself and for the people who were expecting to receive and display them. But then, we must remember that ice is very frail and always dependent on temperature - it needs to be kept very cold to survive. Perhaps we should all remember this fact when contemplating Global Warming .... !

DM

A DOG WITH TWO TALES

Hi, I'm a dog. Before I was a dog, I was human just like you and boy, what a human I was. Drink, drugs, women and fighting, that's what I lived for. Until I had one fight too many. This guy pulls a knife and bingo, out go the lights. Next thing I know I got some doctor leaning over me saying I'm dead and I'm shouting back, you must be crazy. Then I gets this floating feeling and I can see myself lying on a hospital bed, just like in the movies. After that I'm taken off to what I presume was heaven and I'm given all these tests and questions. It was like being interviewed by the cops. Anyway, to cut a long story short the next thing I know is it turns out to be true, the Buddha was right, and I'm re-born as a dog. A crazy dog but still a dog.

My owners are middle-aged people, living on a no-where housing estate in a no-where town. They try their best but they just can't handle me. You see, luckily I have retained most of my human qualities. I still love to cause trouble any way I can and I still love to get into fights. I am a bit disappointed at not being a pure bred – I heard them say I am a Staffy cross Labrador. Perhaps the Buddha or whoever thought it best suited my character.

The woman I live with is easy going. I mean she will shout or yank my chain but that's it, but the guy I got to watch a bit. He can use his hands. It doesn't bother me too much, I got plenty of hidings when I was a human. It ain't too bad being a dog, I mean you get fed regular, it's nice and warm and you get to go out and give the other mutts a hard time. I suppose there might be a bonus as well. I mean after you've been forced to live like a dog the only way is up; right?

In the early days, I got away with lots of stuff. I used to chew everything I could get hold of and they used to say, "Oh, he must be teething." Now though there is always consequences and the question is, am I more willing to do the damage and suffer the old man's beatings anyway?

Yesterday I managed to get away with the third pair of glasses I have stolen off him. I always take them out into the garden, chew on them for a while and then bury them. He is never sure whether I have had them or not. He did know about his new slipper though because he caught me red handed with it in my basket, while I was busy chewing the side out of it. Boy, that was a good beating, but it was worth it because he had only had them two days. I have had three pairs of hers. She is too easy, I mean I just walk up and pull it off her foot and that's it.

The best fun I have is climbing on the furniture, especially if I've just come in from the muddy garden. Then it is a race to get around as many pieces as possible before whoever let me in arrives. I particularly like it in the evenings when they are tired and just want to watch TV. I jump up on the spare settee and lay there while I am shouted at until the old man gets so furious he stands up. Then I jump down looking all meek like. As soon as he sits down, I get up on it again. I can push this for a long time before he explodes.

The other thing I enjoy is chewing through wires. This really does cause excitement. It nearly caused too much excitement, when I chewed through the live wire to the TV and it blew me across the room. I guess I'm not quite as smart as a dog.

Other than that, I spend most of my day taking anything from the house outside into the garden and any rubbish I find in the garden into the house. This infuriates her in particular, especially when I left a dead frog in the kitchen.

I went for a walk with her this morning. I was pulling and jumping about as usual and then I saw another dog approaching. I stared at him with my tail up and he just stared back. I wasn't going to take that, I'm top dog on this estate. I pulled hard with her hanging on and telling me to stop. When I reached the other dog, I grabbed it by the neck and shook it until it was yelping like a baby. Yeh, how do you like that, you little pussy cat.

She managed to pull us apart, but only because I had had enough. The only thing was she just turned around and took me home. I mean, what sort of exercise was that?

When we got in she starts blubbering to the old man about the fight and how she can't control me. Then alarm bells. I hear him say, "This is the end. I'll ring today."

I went to my bed. Perhaps I did go over the top. Who is he ringing? Up to now the worst thing I had thought of was castration, but now, well this was serious. Time for some serious creeping.

I walked back into the living room and brushed against her leg. She just pushed me away. I sat down in front of her and gave her the big sad brown eyes routine.

"Oh, why are like this Ben? You are a naughty boy. Well you've done it this time, daddy's going to find you a new home."

Right, so that's their game. Well, I quite like it here actually. So if he wants to show me off at someone else's house I will eat the first thing I can get my snout on and pee up the wall for good measure.

A few days later, I am loaded in the car. We set off and drive out of town; it dawns on me that this must be it. I am on the back seat, so I move forward between them and I start to bark. After a while she puts her hands over her ears and he begins shouting and swatting at me, but I keep going. About half an hour later, he pulls over.

"If he doesn't stop barking I am going to lock him in the boot," he says.

I decide to keep it down a bit and give them only the occasional burst. In the meantime, I busied myself chewing a hole in the back seat. It was great fun when they realised what I had done. He sent her to sit in the back, which cramped my style a bit so I had to resort to barking again.

Eventually we reached a big house in the country and I saw the sign out front said, "Pet Sanctuary". I don't want no pet sanctuary; I need a warm house with treats and trouble.

I'm dragged into an office while they talk and fill in paper work. Then some woman comes in and takes me. I can see the old man smirking. You won't be smirking when you go back to the car and find I peed on the seat as I left.

She leads me outside and around the back of the house. I can hear what seems like a thousand other dogs barking and whining. There is an enormous run and she takes me in there and lets me off the lead. I am surrounded by wet noses poking where they don't belong. There are some big dogs here too, they come over and push me around. I'm forced to keep my ears down and my tail between my legs, I can't take on this lot. I am the lowest in the pack, even a Yorkshire terrier come over and cocks his leg on me. This is hell and it's cold out here too.

I run over to the edge of the pound and I see my owners driving off. What have I done? I tried to live my doggy life the same as my human life. I didn't learn the lesson. Maybe it's not too late. And if it is, why there is always the next life, ain't there?

BH

BEWARE OF THE CHATTERING MAGPIE

Beware of the chattering magpie,
a very cheeky bird,
Not always to be seen when his
loud cries are heard.
Venture onto his patch and
he soon will have you spotted
From one of the vantage points
that around his home are dotted.
His nest, he builds in thickets,
with a roof to shade his head,
Often lining it with sheep's wool,
to make a comfy bed.
Don't leave your jewellery within
range of his thieving beak

Or given half-a-chance he will
it back home, try to sneak.
Film crews, when outdoors,
with him have to contend,
His rapturous chattering often
drives directors round the bend;
Should the starring role be his,
he never tires of asking,
While other birds quietly sit in
the back-ground basking.
Sadly there's a black side to this cheeky bird,
For when other's nests he raids,
their protests can be heard,
To him their eggs and fledglings are but a tasty meal,
Whilst to his admirers, it quickly dampens his appeal.

GB

THE TABLE WAS TURNED

It was a quiet June Wednesday morning; not many
customers in the store, plenty of time to tidy the exterior
plant department, trees, shrubs, climbers, bedding plants.

"Telephone call for Mr Jonray on line 6." I'm called
Jonray, a combination of my Christian and surname, to
prevent any misunderstanding between staff and customers
as there are a lot of Joneses here.

"Good morning, Mr Jonray speaking. How can I help?"

"Are you the garden centre manager?"

"Yes, that is correct."

"My name is Parton. I purchased a large, oval resin table
ten days ago and it's broken - I'm not impressed."

"You say it's broken? I'm sorry to hear that, could you
explain more?"

"What's to explain. It's broken." I could hear his voice changing tempo. "The table shattered just above one of the legs. Barbeque food, drinks, crockery all over the floor, spoilt our day. You will replace it. I believe it is your company policy and what's more, it is still under guarantee."

While I was listening to him I began checking the delivery schedule and sure enough he had had his table delivered ten days ago and it was one of the most expensive in our range.

"Are you listening to me, Mr Jonray? You don't appear to be paying much attention!"

"Sorry Mr Parton, but I was checking stock availability." I also smelled a rat but I didn't want to let on. "We don't have any of that price because tables of that price are special order only. I shall arrange for the table to be collected and in the meantime I will order you a replacement but it will take about fourteen days."

"You have to be joking. So we can't barbeque for two weeks?"

"I'm sorry but if you had bought a less expensive model I could have replaced it immediately."

I was on my day off when his table materialised in store and when I saw it later my suspicions were confirmed. So I telephoned my supplier's technical department and described the damage to the table. They immediately explained that it was the customer's fault. I thanked them for their help and thought, how do I catch him out?

Fourteen days later on the dot, the replacement table arrived. I checked that every inch of it was as perfect as it could be. I telephoned the customer; his answer phone clicked in. "Mr Parton, it's Mr Jonray - your new table has arrived. I shall be in store for the next four days, please collect it at your leisure."

I was at lunch when he arrived. I had previously instructed my staff to call me when he arrived, so that I could attend to him personally. He stood at the information desk one hand drumming on the polished surface, the other clutching the hand of his little girl aged, I think, between six and seven years. We exchanged pleasantries and then I went to fetch the table. It was, thankfully, where I had put it and untouched. I carried it to the desk and apologised again. One of my staff had brought him a flat bed trolley and he began to place his table on it. Once finished he began to say something but I ignored him, turned to his daughter and crouched low.

Then I said to her, "And you be more careful next time."

"No," she exclaimed, "it wasn't me. My daddy hit it with a wine bottle." I smiled as he yanked his daughter's hand and struggled out of the store.

RJ

FAREWELL TO A FALLEN SHEEP

Inverted its body lies, its life expired,
The battle lost, the flesh worn and tired,
The hours of pain and suffering past,
Its soul released to roam at last;
To wander over hill and dale,
Through gentle rain and stinging hail,
Warmed by sun, cooled by dew,
Free to graze in pastures new;
Ready to answer the shepherd's call
For all his creatures, great and small,
To return to his heavenly fold
From this world, harsh and cold.

GB

A FISHERMAN'S TALE

The sun shone down on the harbour, the sun's rays
reflecting off the sea; James squinted into the glare.
He ambled towards the pier, which pointed out to sea like
an accusing finger and saw his father's fishing boat coming
into view.

"Blimey, here we go," he said as he continued, head
bowed and hands thrust into his ragged jeans pockets.

When he reached the end of the pier, his father was
already mooring the boat. James looked down at the piles
of crab pots stacked on the deck and resigned himself to
the work ahead. He watched his father climb the vertical
ladder; he had done this many times himself and knew it
was tough but his father showed no sign of strain as he
climbed steadily towards him.

"Now then," his father said as he hauled himself up,
brushing the dirt from his hands. "I don't suppose you've
done anything yet?"

"I've only just got here," James said, kicking a pebble over
the side.

"Oh, just got out of bed I suppose. Don't know what
you'll do when you take this business over – b****y crabs
won't wait all day for you to shift your backside." James did
not reply, he knew it was pointless to argue and he was sick
of trying to get through to him. "I don't want to be a
b****y fisherman," he said to himself.

He had been trying to tell his father this for years but he
would not listen, he was so stubborn he refused to hear it.
"There are no other jobs here. Craster is a village, you'd
have to move to the city and you wouldn't last two minutes
there," he would say.

"You can empty them pots; I'm off to the pub. I'll be

back later and you can come out with me in the boat. That's if your diary is free."

James watched him walk away. He stared hatefully at his departing figure as though his thoughts could burn a hole in his father's back.

James set about the work, climbing back and forth between the boat and the pier sorting the meagre catch. He began throwing down pots and kicking ropes, his temper just contained. When he had finished he sat on the edge of the pier, legs dangling, and looked out to sea. A storm was coming. The grey clouds moved across the horizon and the wind started to pull at his dark tousled hair. The sea was choppy now and he did not fancy going out in a rough sea.

"Sitting about again?"

He turned and saw Dave Williams standing behind him. They had gone to school together but that was where the likeness ended. Dave was good at everything. He was good at sports, good with women and a good boathand. He bragged about getting a boat of his own but couldn't so he spent his time trying to impress James's father and usually succeeding.

"Don't you start; I've had enough from the old man. Anyway I've done everything he wanted, all I have to do now is go with him this afternoon."

"You're going?" he asked, with ill disguised disbelief.

"Yes, I'm going. It'll be my boat one day, or so he keeps insisting."

"Well, if you can't handle it, I know someone who can." James said nothing. Part of him wished he would take the damn boat but the jealous streak in him refused to let it go.

It was late afternoon when his father returned.

"Hello, Dave, looking for a trip?"

When his father spoke James smelled a mixture of tobacco and beer fumes. His nose wrinkled and he felt himself recoil.

"Well if James isn't coming," Dave replied.

"What do you mean, 'not coming?' Of course he's coming. Why, what's he said?"

James shot Dave a reproachful glance, silently thanking him for dropping him in it.

"Err, I was just thinking if Dave was going, then I needn't bother."

"Just typical, you're going and that's it," his father said.

Dave smiled sweetly and said, "If I'm in the way?"

"No, no, you're welcome, we always need a good hand. Isn't that right James?"

"Yeah," he replied through clenched teeth.

They left the harbour and headed towards the darkening clouds. The wind had picked up now and waves broke over the bow and sprayed over the wheelhouse into James' face stinging his eyes. He found himself gripping the handrail while watching Dave working among the ropes and pots, seemingly oblivious to the swell.

"Why can't I be like him?" he thought.

His father glanced back at Dave and James knew he was thinking the same.

When they reached the crab ground, Dave sprang into action. James made an effort to help but Dave kept moving him out of the way and reached most of the pots before him. They worked for almost an hour and James felt soaked, cold, and miserable.

His father cut the engines and the boat immediately began to rise and fall in the swell.

"You alright boy? You look a bit green."

"I'm okay," James lied.

His father emerged from the wheelhouse unscrewing the lid from a flask and balancing in the swell.

James watched his father drink the steaming liquid from the plastic cup. "I hope it b***ding chokes you," he said under his breath.

The sea was getting rough now and he wished his father would start the engines and move on.

His father finished his drink, shook the cup empty and turned towards the wheelhouse.

"At last," James murmured.

His father took a couple of steps, then a wave struck the side of the boat slewing it over. James hit the deck and as he did he saw his father flying across the boat, both feet off the ground and hit head first against the gunnel with a sickening crunch.

"Ah-h-h," Dave said, getting up.

James got to his feet and ran to his father's motionless body. A large wound had opened on his scalp and blood formed a growing puddle on the deck.

"Dad, dad, can you hear me?" There was no reply.

"Is he alive?" Dave said.

James felt a faint pulse.

"There's a first aid kit in the wheelhouse. Get it!"

Dave ran to the wheelhouse without questioning and emerged with a small green box.

James opened the box, tearing at the packaging and held some swabs to the gaping wound. Blood quickly oozed through the swabs and ran down his hands.

"It's no good, you can't stop it. He's gonna die, isn't he?" Dave said.

"Just get us back ashore," James snapped.

"I can't! I don't know how to start the engines. I've never been in the wheelhouse," he said.

James looked at him and couldn't resist a dig. "I thought you wanted to be a skipper?"

James packed more swabs into the wound and secured them with a bandage.

"Keep pressure on the wound," he said.

"Where did you learn this?" Dave asked.

"I didn't learn it. It's common sense."

James went to the wheelhouse. It took a few minutes to get his bearings. He had seen his father start the boat many times but he had never been interested enough to do it for himself. He carefully primed the engine and turned the key.

To his great relief, a large grey plume of exhaust smoke rose from the stern and the engine came to life. Turning the boat he pushed the throttles forward until the noise was deafening and headed for the shore.

"I can't stop the blood."

James turned and saw the dishevelled figure of Dave standing in the doorway. His face was ashen and blood dripped from his hands.

"Look, take over. Just steer west and keep the throttle open," he said, pushing past Dave.

He crouched by his father's body.

"Don't you die, you old pirate," he said.

He tied the rest of the bandages around his father's head and returned to the wheelhouse.

"I'll take her now," he said.

"What am I supposed to do?" Dave said.

"Just hold his b****y hand if you can't do anything else," James snapped.

The journey back took a lifetime, but had only been forty minutes. James had managed to raise the alarm on the V.H.F. radio and blue lights flickered on the harbour wall. They moored and the paramedic came aboard and attended to his father.

"Will he be all right?" James asked.

The paramedic placed an oxygen mask on his father,. then turned and said, "I think so, it will depend on the x-ray results. You did a good job with the bandages."

They loaded his father into the ambulance and James climbed in next to him. After a few minutes he saw him slowly open his eyes and look around.

"Where the hell am I?" he croaked.

"You had an accident, luckily it was only your head. You've been out for over an hour," James replied.

"Dave got me back, did he?"

"No, Dave was useless; I got you back."

His father looked at him for a while and then said, "I told you I would make a fisherman of you." James held his father's hand and said, "Yeah, perhaps or maybe a paramedic."

BH

SPELLBINDER

In the rain
a fairy princess walks
in a magical gown.
Tall stone buildings either side
with empty eyes, stare down
enchanted, as she glides
like a white lamp
spreading warmth on the damp
dull people passing by.
Mother strides beside her
pram-pushing a baby prince.
Shadows march in front
reflected, stunted in the rain,
but tall guarding small.
Holding the handle tight
like a magic wand, again
she hopes that special night
of promises will all
come true.
The crown on high-held-head
glitters in the grey morning.
Is there stardust being shed
on the wet ground?
A sad man smiles
catching that sparkle
spinning around.
No carriages today.
She walks
with mother
in the rain.

JS

THE GIFT

Tom Harrold was twelve years old, loved trains and like lots of boys of his day, dreamt of being a train driver when he left school. Steam trains, he thought, had style and character and he secretly hoped he might be fortunate enough to work with them one day. He had his own Hornby double '0' gauge railway layout in the cellar of his home and spent many a long hour setting out the track and making models for the scenery. He was also very knowledgeable about steam trains and constantly had his head in some book or other from the library learning as much as he could about his favourite subject.

It was 1951. His father had walked out on the marriage when he was eight years old and his mother had taken several part-time jobs to keep their home going. One of the people his mother kept house for was a middle-aged gentleman who lived near Chesham. When she first started working at Mr Lawrence's house, he specified that he would not want her to bother with one of the upstairs bedrooms. The door to the room was kept locked and although she often wondered why, politeness forbade her to ask such a question. Often, whilst at the house, Mr Lawrence would invite her to sit and have a cup of tea with him and he would always enquire after young Tom, showing a keen interest in his well-being and his interest in trains.

Then, one Sunday his mother announced to Tom that Mr Lawrence was coming to have tea with them. Not having many visitors these days, Tom was quite excited at the prospect of him coming; besides, his mother had mentioned that Mr. Lawrence was also interested in railways so they would have something to talk about together. After they had eaten their meal, Tom took Mr Lawrence down into the cellar to take a look at the railway layout which was set out on raised boards. After discussing the expansive layout with him, they spent time running the trains and Mr Lawrence complimented Tom on his knowledge and skill in model making. The lad proudly explained how one day he would like to drive a real steam train!

As Mr Lawrence was leaving he asked Mrs Harrold if she would accompany him with Tom to Beaconsfield the following Sunday. He was sure the young lad would appreciate seeing the model trains that ran through the scenic layout at Beckonscot Village, there. From then on, this trip became a regular treat for Tom as he and Mr Lawrence shared the interest of model railways together.

Fast forward fifteen years, and Tom together with his wife, Sue, and his mother are sitting in Mr Lawrences' house. During the intervening years they had become very close, resulting in Mrs Harrold and Tom moving in with the kindly gentleman. There had been no relationship as such between himself and Mrs Harrold, save a unique friendship, which had allowed her and young Tom a secure home-life with him. Sadly, Mr Lawrence had recently passed away and a letter from his solicitor addressed to them both had arrived that morning. Tom looked at the large brown envelope on the table. Tearing it open, he took out the hand-written letter and began reading it to his mother:

Dear Mrs Harrold and Tom,

Over the years you have been very kind to me, taking care of my needs and filling this once quiet house with laughter again. Mrs Harrold, I leave this house to you, Tom and Sue with my love and gratitude for all you have done for me. I trust you will continue to enjoy living here .

I need to explain to you now that I was once married to a beautiful lady called Rosemary and she bore me a son. I adored her and was devastated when she tragically died of a kidney failure in 1950. This was to be a double tragedy for me, as our son Joseph had also passed away at a young age some years previously. He was born with a severe disability and could do little for himself. However, as a little boy he loved trains, and I built a layout in his bedroom upstairs. We would spend hours together as he watched me build the scenery, unable to participate in the process except by offering wonderful smiles as I completed yet another building or wild shrieks of laughter as the trains went round the track at such high speed they almost derailed!

When he died, I couldn't bring myself to use the layout again, so I simply packed it away and locked the door on his room. In your wisdom, dear Mrs Harrold, you never questioned why that had been so and I thank you for that.

Tom, you helped to fill an awful void in my life, allowing me to share your interest in model trains whilst you were growing up. I have had the privilege of seeing you mature into an intelligent and interesting young man who now has a wonderful and caring wife. You certainly have an exciting future ahead of you! Driving a diesel train is a very skilful job, so well done for achieving your ambition to become a train driver. Now, I would like to bequeath to you the railway layout in my sons' bedroom (the key for which is enclosed). I know that you will take care of the trains and hopefully share them with children of your own one day.

Thank you for making a lonely old man very happy again! God Bless you all,

With my fondest love, Mr Arthur Lawrence.

JC

ONE GOOD TURN
DESERVES ANOTHER

The elderly, shabbily dressed lady was obviously looking for
something or somebody as she studied the lane intently.
She was standing in the entrance of a garage, one of several
that backed onto the lane. Minutes passed and she
appeared a little agitated, but then a small figure turned
into the lane from the main road. She also was elderly,
dressed in old-fashioned clothing, and carrying several bags
of different descriptions. The two women obviously knew
each other and greeted one another with a hug.

"Evening, Pam," said the late arrival. "I was beginning to
wonder whether I would be able to find you, not knowing
the area."

"Well, I did say it was well past the pub, didn't I?" replied
Pam. The two women entered the garage, Ellen breathing a
sigh of relief that she had at last reached her destination.
She hadn't known where her friend lived exactly; in fact all
she knew about her was that she always seemed cheerful
and in good health.

"Never mind, dear, you're here now. Sit down in that
little armchair and make yourself comfortable. I'll soon
make us a nice cup of tea."

Ellen looked round the garage in amazement. There in
one corner was a small armchair, the one Pam had
suggested she sit on; along one wall was a washing
machine, tumble dryer, a cooker and an electric fire.
It didn't look much like a garage!

"You're very snug here, aren't you? How on earth did all
this come about?" Ellen enquired, naturally puzzled with
the surroundings.

Whilst Pam was making the tea, she started to explain.

"Well, one day whilst I was traipsing around in the rain, this lady just collapsed in front of me; she clean passed out. I thought she had fainted but it turned out she'd collapsed because she had diabetes and had gone too long without food. No-one seemed to notice, except me.

"When I bent over her she whispered to me something about sugar or sweets - that she needed them urgently. I raked through my old flight bag and gave her a couple of sugar lumps that I'd sneaked from the cafe on the front a few days earlier. She seemed to improve after that, and was so grateful I had stopped to help her. I asked her where she lived and managed to get her home safely."

"What happened next?" enquired Ellen impatiently.

"Well, she kept saying how much she appreciated my help; that, if I hadn't been there for her she might well have gone into a coma and died. Said I'd saved her life; that she'd never be able to repay me. I told her she owed me nothing but she insisted I stop with her for a cup of tea. We got talking and when she found out that I didn't actually live anywhere special, she said she didn't like the idea of me being out in all weathers and not having a roof over my head at night. She said she couldn't offer me a home with her but, as she no longer had a car and didn't need a garage, I would be very welcome to use it for sleeping in.

"Of course I explained that her offer wasn't really necessary, but Mrs. P. is a very persuasive lady and eventually I agreed to her suggestion.

"She took me down the garden and into the garage via a side-door, and I must say I was flabbergasted to see the interior. Mrs. P. said that her husband had made good use of the garage during his lifetime but once he had passed away it was used just for storage. So, when she purchased a new washing machine-cum-tumble dryer, the older equipment found its way into the garage. The electric fire had been used by her husband on colder mornings when he'd felt like making an early start."

"What about the electric cooker?" Ellen enquired.

"Well, there again, Mr. P. bought herself a more up-to-date model so the older one became obsolete and finished up down here."

"So, what happened next? What did the lady actually say?" asked Ellen.

"Here's your tea, dear," said Pam, handing her friend a steaming cup of tea and a plate of biscuits. "Drink it while it's nice and hot."

She continued: "Well, Mrs. P. suggested I make myself comfortable in her garage during the hours of darkness. She wouldn't interfere with my way of life providing I didn't make a mess or a lot of noise. And, as the garage was wired up for electricity, I could make myself something hot each night before I went to bed and before I left in the morning. She also said that as she was entitled to cheaper electricity, I wasn't to worry if I needed to put the little fire on occasionally.

"Are you ready for another cup?" she asked her friend. "Do you like ginger cake? Mrs. P. gave it to me the other day and I put it in the fridge to keep it fresh."

"A fridge as well," exclaimed Ellen. "I suppose that also arrived in the same way as the other things." She passed her cup for a refill.

"You're right there, dear," Pam replied. "For example, there were two nice sunbeds, with mattresses, which Mrs. P. said I could use. She told me she had found them very comfortable during the days when she used to sunbathe. Would you like a piece of cake?" Not waiting for a reply,

Pam proceeded to cut two slices for each of the plates she had laid out in readiness.

As the two women began to consume their cake, Ellen continue to study the interior of the garage. Right down the far end she saw a little unit, the sort that are installed in cottages or small premises. It comprised a sink on one side with a draining-board on the other and underneath was a cupboard, and opposite to that three drawers. Next to the unit was a small cupboard with another set of drawers.

Ellen couldn't wait until she had finished eating her cake before remarking, "Do you know, Pam, this place is just like a furnished flatlet. You really have fallen on your feet; you've got everything you need here except a loo, of course."

"Oh, that's O.K." Pam replied. "I do have access to a loo because, apparently, Mr. P. was a very fastidious man and when he had finished gardening or tinkering he always visited the loo, washed his hands and, apparently, always changed his shoes before going into the house. So, if you turn left from the side-door you'll see an outdoor W.C. which he had built onto the garage. The water pipes supply the loo and my little sink in here. How's that for 'All Mod. Cons'?" They both chuckled at the corny joke.

Still gobsmacked, Ellen asked, "How do you manage to pay for things, you know - like your tea, sugar and milk? I've never seen you begging."

"Well, dear, I've always got my Post Office savings book with me to depend on. Mind, in the old days I used to keep it well tucked away at night-times, for safety, but now I just hide it somewhere in here when I'm not going to use it.

"You know, it wasn't until my husband died that I discovered he was quite a rich man - although you would never have thought it during his lifetime; always very frugal he was. When the solicitor was sorting out our affairs, I told him I would prefer my money to be paid to me in instalments instead of a lump sum, so he drew up what he loosely referred to as an annuity. Also, I told him I wasn't sure where I would be living once the lease on our flat had expired, and that this would be quite soon. So I arranged with him to send me a cheque each month, c/o the local Post Office, for the time being, and that if I left the area I would inform him so that he would know where to send payments in future. That was four years ago. The money arrives each month and the arrangement suits me, so I haven't been in touch with him since.

"I really dont know how long the money will last; it was supposed to be a long-term agreement. When the money runs out, then I'll consider my options, but until then I try to enjoy life. Of course, since I've lived here, for the past year or so now, life has been really cushy."

"Why didn't you get another flat after your husband's death? What made you decide to change your lifestyle?" Ellen asked.

Pam gave some thought to her friend's question before replying.

"Well, I suppose I was a bit bored with life. I felt I had never achieved anything, not even done anything really. I thought I'd like to see how the other half lived. Mind, it was hard at first. Luckily, I started in the summer so sleeping out-of-doors wasn't too bad; but when winter came I began to think I'd made a big mistake and was considering looking for a flat or cottage. But I'd made some very nice, genuine friends, and the freedom to think and do as I liked was very appealing; so I stuck it out and gradually it became a natural way of life to me."

Ellen was obviously impressed by her friend's revelations. "Well, I think things have worked out really great for you. This might be only a garage to some people but it's a real 'Home from Home!' for you," she said.

Taking a deep breath, Pam responded in a serious manner.

"Actually, Ellen, I've brought you here to ask you something. I don't know how you are going to take it but, since your arthritis is getting so much worse, don't you think it's time you stopped sleeping rough? I know you're a free spirit and all that but really I think you need somewhere warm and comfortable now. Sleeping in a shelter on the front isn't too bad in the summer but, as I know from personal experience, nights can be very cold and draughty in the winter. And when it's wet weather you must be in permanently damp clothes."

"But what alternative do I have?" replied Ellen. "My family, such as it is, do not want to know anything about me these days; they've climbed the social ladder and become middle class."

Pam continued: "Well, Mrs. P. had a word with me the other day. She suggested that perhaps I might like to have some company here. She said providing things continued to run as smoothly as they had done so far, she would not mind if I invited a friend to live here with me, to share my accommodation, especially during the winter months. So – what do you think dear? Would you be interested in becoming my 'flatmate'?"

Ellen was overcome by this invitation and tears began to flow from her wizened eyes. "But are you sure I'm the right person?" she enquired of Pam.

"I have known you for many years now, dear, and in all of that time I have never known you to be unkind or complaining. I'm sure we will get on very well together. So tonight we'll open up both of the campbeds, and I've got sufficient blankets for the two of us."

And so they settled down for a warm and comfortable night, and many happy months together.

Two years later, Mrs. P. passed away. During this time she had met Ellen and taken to her and was glad that Pam had someone like-minded for company.

When the Will was read, it transpired that Mrs. P's house was to be inherited by Pam, together with a quite substantial sum of money. Apparently Mr. P. had been a Bank Manager and had made ample provision for his wife. His solicitor, as the executor of the Will, had been instructed to take care of all outgoing expenses incurred by his wife.

There was just one clause of an obligatory nature in the Will. It read:

"In view of the fact that Pam Brown saved my life in 1999, when I collapsed as a result of diabetes, I am leaving to her all that I own on my death – the only proviso being that she move into my house with a friend and live there for the duration of her life and that she find another tenant for her present abode."

Pam and Ellen did in fact move into the big house, and they soon found new tenants for their 'flatlet' - at no rent, of course.

So, who can doubt the truth in the saying that "One good turn deserves another", or alternatively "What goes round, comes round."

DM

REFLECTIONS OF LIFE

It had been two years now since Maggie had moved away from her family to live by the sea. The day she told her children of her plans still haunted her. The look on their faces of utter disbelief and sadness that she would no longer be just around the corner, but miles away from them, was awful.

"I need to be Maggie Stuart, not just your mother and a granny," she had said. "This move will hopefully allow me to do just that. I feel I want to be independent, live my own life and find the real me again. I know it's hard for you but please try to understand."

After all, her children were in fact grown up with families of their own. They led their own busy lives now and called by to their mother at the weekend for Sunday lunch. Routinely, they would talk of their week whilst the grandchildren walked the dogs and then curled up in front of the TV. Typically, whatever they watched, they were engrossed until it was time to leave again.

The grandchildren had loved being with their granny when they were small. She took them for long walks and played with them at the park. Maggie always made cakes with them and allowed them to make a mess with finger-paint – something their parents definitely did not. But now they were older life was different and somewhat disconnected from the elderly lady they affectionately called their granny.

When the grandchildren were born Maggie asked to be called 'granny' rather than 'nanny.' She didn't feel old then and was so proud to be a granny. Now she looked in the mirror and saw her own mother looking back at her. She had started to become the elderly granny she had not planned to be. In her mind she still felt young yet life was indeed slipping by too fast. She had loved her life so far – she had been truly blessed with a lovely family but still hankered after unfulfilled dreams. She had wrestled with this yearning for some time but a voice inside her now told her to follow those dreams before it was too late.

Maggie had cared for someone for most of her life. First, as a teenager, for her brothers and sisters whilst her parents worked and then later bringing up her own family. It had not been easy lately, alone, after forty-two years of marriage and emotionally she had found it all too much at times. But still, here she was with two wonderful children and five adoring grandchildren.

"Why on earth you want to move so far away beggars belief," her children had said. "When will we see you now? School holidays and Christmas, we suppose, but it won't be the same. You do realise how much we'll miss you, don't you, Mum?" "Of course it will be difficult for us all but you just have to understand that this is something I must do before it's too late," she'd said, "so, although I will miss you all very much we can talk on the phone and I shall come back to visit you and you must come to stay with me."

Very reluctantly, they gave their blessing and now two years on they saw a new woman in their mother and granny. She had a stride in her step that they had never witnessed before and her face glowed with a contentment that had evaded her for many a year.

The peacefulness she found in that quiet, friendly seaside village was wonderful and the comfortable solitude she experienced, immeasurable.

Now, her teenage grandchildren really enjoyed their visits and instead of immersing themselves in the television as before they would happily join their granny on those long walks by the seashore and talk interestingly of all they had done since they last saw her.

Today it was the anniversary of her husband's death and Maggie took a walk by the sea, alone with her thoughts.

Autumn was just around the corner and the winds whipped the seashore scattering the sand across her path. The sun was trying to break through the low cloud and as it did so it lit up the shoreline.

She looked across the beach to see a young boy desperately trying to launch his bright orange kite into the skies. Seagulls soared overhead and swooped down in search of tasty morsels amongst the seashells as the tide

moved its grey waters relentlessly to and fro. The roaring
sound of the sea was broken momentarily by the sound of
children's laughter.

Memories for Maggie of times gone by when she too
traced her children's names in the wet sand and built
sandcastles with them both returned as she watched these
youngsters playing with their parents. She walked past rows
of deserted beach-huts that only weeks ago were alive with
the chatter of conversation and clutter of deck chairs
and tea mugs. They were silenced now by the

autumn's emptiness.

The holiday season over, local residents walked their dogs by the seashore, shifting the same sands each day with their footprints that the tide would take away on its return. Come rain or shine their four-legged companions had nudged them from their comfy armchairs to take them for a walk and today their owners were trying to quicken their step under the gathering clouds.

Maggie stood as she always did to take in this sight that never failed to uplift her spirits. The seasons through it were forever breathtaking. A sandy beach as far as the eye could see and mighty waters stretching out to where they met the skies. Wonderful, she thought to herself, standing there alone in her own little world, this really is heaven on earth! She considered herself very fortunate and had always loved this view from the moment she first saw it all those years ago.

She so missed her husband still, but within the huge loss of him she had at last found a peace and contentment she never knew existed. For a brief moment within the stillness of her heart, she felt the closeness of her husband, and she was lost in her thoughts of him.

She glanced across the beach and saw that the boy had managed to launch his kite. The children with their parents ran around the sand laughing together with not a care in the world.

At long last, Maggie had reached the stage in her life she thought was beyond her wildest dreams and she was truly content. She walked briskly back to her little cottage that overlooked the sea. At any time of the day now she could have this amazing view that warmed her from top to toe and it made her feel so complete.

That evening she phoned her family as she always did.

They had heard her say it a thousand times before but it made them smile as always to know their mother had begun to live the life she had always dreamed of.

As Maggie spoke she caught a glimpse of herself in the hall mirror. Within the reflection was always now, her mother looking back at her. And yet for a second, she thought she saw a glimpse of Maggie, the youthful woman, and it made her smile. Life was good, she thought.

JC

COWARDLY RETRIBUTION

Such an insignificant beginning ... a small piece of rag, soaked in lighter fuel, caught alight and hastily pushed through a letterbox.

But on contact with the floor it burst into a miriad of sparks, causing flames to run along the combustible carpet, licking hungrily at the skirting boards in the hall. From there it quickly mounted the papered walls, swiftly engulfing the door-frames, while thick, choking smoke began to fill the air. No chance of any early warning; the alarm's battery had long since run its course.

Within minutes the flames had reached a downstairs room where the curtains and old-fashioned furniture immediately caught fire. The extreme heat caused the television screen to implode, mirrors and glassware to shatter, and angry flames to quickly consume the carpeting and everything else in the room.

With nothing to impede its progress, the fire soon reached other downstairs rooms, inflicting maximum damage and rendering them useless. Fierce flames mounted the stairs and relentlessly advanced into the bedrooms.

Escape through the upstairs windows was investigated but because double-glazing is not conducive to breakage, it did not yield to the occupants' frantic efforts to retreat from the intense heat and choking smoke into the fresh air and safety.

Eventually, thick smoke engulfed the whole of the house, choking all those inside. Their coughing and frantic screams for help went unheard, drowned by the roar of the now rampant flames. Both people and animals were overcome; all collapsed and died from smoke inhalation, well before their bodies were burned almost beyond recognition.

It would eventually be decided that the multiple deaths were due to "the illegal actions of a person or persons unknown"; little solace to friends and relatives who were left bewildered and grieving.

An insignificant beginning had culminated in a terrible and tragic end ... a small piece of cloth, soaked in an inflammable substance, lit by a single match and pushed through a letterbox had resulted in so much heartache and damage. And for what? Revenge? Maybe.

A catastrophe which was devastating to so many had been so easy to bring about. But how can humankind be so callous? (And it usually happened to the most vulnerable of people.) Was it an action brought about by hatred, religious intolerance, jealousy or just plain vandalism. Even considered to be 'a lark'.

FIRE ... it can be such a terrible weapon, and have so many repercussions.

DM

UN-POSTED LETTERS

Farmer David Jones, Davy to his friends, replaced the phone and breathed a sigh of relief. "The vet will be with you within the hour," he had been told reassuringly. When Sally, his favourite cow, began having trouble calving Davy knew it was time to call for professional help. He had phoned the vets knowing that Harry Swain, his regular vet and lifelong friend was unavailable.

Walking across the kitchen to stoke the fire, Davy's eyes focused on the faded envelope that stood in the centre of the mantle-piece. Thirty years had passed since he'd written that letter; each time when he moved it he wondered about how she would have reacted, had it been posted. Theirs had been a classical boy and girl-next-door romance. Susan's father had farmed the next farm down the lane. They had talked about becoming engaged when she turned eighteen. Just before her eighteenth birthday her father sold the farm and all the family had moved to another farm two hundred miles away. Shortly after their move, Davy's father had died and all his energies had gone into looking after his mother, Julia, his sister and their farm.

He had written the letter when Susan refused to answer his weekly phone-calls and all correspondence from her had stopped. After dithering for weeks over posting the letter, he finally decided he had left it too late but could not bring himself to burn it.

Davy hadn't looked at anyone else after Susan's departure, spending his time looking after the farm and the family. Their mother sadly had passed away shortly before his sister's marriage by which time he had become a confirmed bachelor.

Having built-up the fire he went across the yard to try

once again to calm Sally. Shortly to his relief he heard a vehicle skid to a stop and he rushed outside calling, "Over here," on seeing a fair-haired young man pulling on green Wellingtons.

"I'm Charlie Benton, Harry Swain's locum vet. I take it you're David Jones?"

"Yes. You certainly weren't long getting here. I assume you've got satellite navigation in your vehicle as this isn't the easiest farm in the district to find?"

"Better than that, I've got a driver who knows the area well; she used to live around here years ago."

Together they entered the cowshed where the young vet gave Sally an internal examination, skilfully gripping a pair of calf's legs as he withdrew his arm.

There was something about Charlie that Davy liked, whether it was his calmness or the way the cow had responded to him. All Davy knew for certain was that within twenty minutes of arriving he had delivered Sally's calf.

After making sure the calf was alright Charlie asked if he could wash and clean-up. As they walked to the farmhouse he said, "A cup of tea would be appreciated. I'm sure my driver would love one too as we left in rather a hurry."

After showing Charlie where to wash, Davy placed the kettle on the fire and informed him he was going to fetch his driver. Approaching Charlie's Landrover he heard one of his favourite tunes being played. A tap on the side window caused the driver to turn. Davy froze as she wound down the window; he couldn't believe his eyes. The driver was no other than his old flame Susan. She still looked the same as she did in the photograph that stood on the mantle-piece.

"Charlie thought you would be ready for a cup of tea and a biscuit," he gasped, as he opened the Landrover's door.

Before Susan had a chance to speak the heavens opened, making them run for the shelter of the farmhouse. Once inside, Susan made for the roaring fire while Davy busied himself making a pot of tea. Charlie, seated at the kitchen table, watched as Susan looked around the room. She stopped when she saw her photograph on the mantle-piece with the envelope propped against it.

"May I have a look what's inside?" she asked after seeing her name written in faded writing.

Davy thought long and hard. "Yes, I would like you to read the letter inside. After all this time I still mean what's written."

Susan reached for the envelope, carefully unfolded the letter inside and started reading. Tears rolled down her cheeks long before she reached the end. Charlie rose from his seat, crossed the room and hugged her. "Are you alright, mother?"

"I'll be fine in minute, son. If only your father had posted his letter thirty years ago our lives could have been so very different."

Davy stood transfixed. Charlie his son! He couldn't believe what Susan had just said. He wanted to say something but couldn't find any words to describe his feelings.

Charlie broke the silence. "What a stupid pair I've got for parents. You father, for writing down your feelings but never posting the letter. On the other hand, mother, I've watched you transferring a crumpled letter from one handbag to another. There's no name on the envelope but I guessed, sometime ago, that it was meant for my father. Am I right?"

"I'm sorry to say, yes. I think that after reading his letter I ought to give him this," she replied fumbling in the depths of her handbag.

Davy crossed the room and took a tattered envelope from her shaking hand. Twice he read the letter, his expressions not giving any clues to what thoughts were going through his mind. When he finally finished reading he moved forward and grasped Susan tightly. The embrace that followed told Charlie that before long he would be walking his mother down the aisle.

GB

LIFE'S PASSION SPENT

Stone faced,
The old man sits
Motionless,
Hands clasped,
Head draped low.
Youth's prime
Long past,
Mind recalling
Opportunities missed,
Chances taken.
Tears like mists
Cloud the eyes,
Death's cold grip
Slowly encompassing
His worn-out body,
No resistance offered,
Life's passion spent.

GB

THE POSTAGE STAMP

Trepidation engulfed him as he entered the courtroom. He was 27, 6'1" of medium build, nothing special to look at, but he hoped his suited appearance would hold sway with the judge's decision.

He shivered – was it the cold, crisp February morning, or was it because he was in an area of unknown territory?

His solicitor presented some evidence and then he took his stand in the witness box, and told his side of the story.

On returning to his seat the bench left the room. He stared around the room, unable to take in what he saw and spoke only little to his learned friend beside him. Then the interminable wait, one that will never be forgotten.

He started to the sound of "all rise". He thought he could not move. "You have been awarded custody of your two children." He cried, his wish fulfilled. "With maintenance of £5 per week per child." The money was the last thing on his mind. "Your wife has been granted reasonable access." He did not know why she did not contest the case. Then he left, a wiser but emotionally drained man.

A year passed. Life was hard but very rewarding, and the maintenance destined to pay for his children's child minder never really materialised, and with arrears steadily mounting, the court intervened.

Trepidation engulfed him again as he entered the court room only this time he was not totally in awe of his surroundings. Case heard, he gathered his thoughts – again another nail biting wait. "You have been awarded £5 per child per year with all arrears remitted." On this occasion his wife contested the case and in person.

Christmas came and he still had found no way to make the b***h pay. It is one of those times when children send cards to their mothers although, on this occasion, God knows why.

He entered his local post office, envelope in hand and started to walk to the counter. Only yards from it he stopped, turned and retraced his footsteps, the bemused assistant calling as he left the premises.

He placed the addressed envelope into the post box, minus its stamp. She will have to pay now, he smiled.

RJ

MANDIBLE

Crunch, crunch. Golden arches swallow up
the corner shop.
Munch, munch gobbles the multi-million-dollar
store as it eats
the little café in its massive jaw.
Crush the small —
the post office, all the terraced houses
chop, spew out flats and paving stones
and grey concrete blocks.
Take away the village school,
build
a campus for three thousand souls,
each a number on a role, anonymous.
Pounce and eat,
you grinding mandible
if you see green.
But, don't forget —
Save The Planet

JS

CONTENTMENT

When I gaze through my window
what do I see?
Hundreds of chickens
running free.
And dozens of rabbits
chasing around;
Scratching or nibbling,
they're making no sound.

I can look out on fields
with hedges and trees;
From whatever direction
I catch every breeze.
In the distance a farmhouse
is lit up all night;
While occasional traffic
generates moving light.

I wonder at cloud-shapes,
colour and form;
And gaze enraptured
when sunsets perform.
I know I am lucky I'll
never object
To living in the country
My life's just perfect.

DM

CHANCE ENCOUNTERS

Judith and Simon sat together in Suzie's Pantry drinking coffee, watching the world go by. They knew from personal experience that nothing in this seaside town went unnoticed. No matter how long you lived there, soon enough everyone knew who you were or thought they did, but then, that was par for the course for the retired population of Waterford Bay.

Smiling at Simon, Judith reflected on how she'd been introduced to the coffee shop by Jesse, her neighbour, when they'd stopped in the high street for a chat one day, not long after Judith had moved from the midlands to the coast. "Do you fancy joining me for a cuppa? I'll show you a lovely cafe, come on." With that, she'd grabbed Judith's arm, crossed the road and headed towards 'Suzie's Pantry' next to the Gift shop and alongside the White Cliff Hotel.

"How are you settling in? Beginning to find your way around now?" she had enquired. "You'll find everyone very friendly here, and there's always something happening to make you smile. You never know, you might be sitting here one day, and in will walk the man of your dreams," she joked as they took a table together by the counter. "And pigs might fly!" laughed Judith loudly, who had been happily single for some years with no intention of starting a new relationship.

After that initial visit, Judith generally popped in after doing her shopping on a Friday. The cafe was usually busy from about eleven, as customers came in for morning coffee and then lunches, so she tried to get there as early as possible to enable her to have a table to herself. Over the months she had begun to get to know the characters that lived in the village and with time on her hands she loved nothing more than reading a few pages of a magazine and drinking her coffee whilst observing the comings and goings. It was definitely the place where people came together to enjoy a cuppa and chat and Jesse was right – whatever time of day, there was always something going on and somebody to talk to. "I'll have a scone with my coffee today please, Carol," she said to the waitress as she took a seat near the counter.

The proud owners of two King Charles spaniels, Bert and Liz, always came into the cafe in the morning after walking their dogs. Rumour had it that they were on the beach with them every morning by six o'clock whatever the weather. Their lives revolved around their dogs but with no family nearby, their four-legged friends were their priority now. Friday was their day for meeting with another elderly couple who were also dog-owners. Since moving Judith had come to the conclusion that retirement and dogs went hand in hand and Bert and Liz were living proof that owning a pet not only kept one occupied but incredibly healthy too. Contrary to her family's opinion, moving away was the best thing she'd done in a long time and she was far from lonely. Given time though, she thought she might consider a canine companion in her old age.

Glancing up from her magazine Judith saw Mrs Charteris, Chair of the Ladies Luncheon Club, across the street. With not a wisp of her neat grey hair out of place and dressed smartly in designer jacket and high heeled patent shoes she carried out her shopping with great efficiency. Moving swiftly between the green grocers and the butchers she handed the purchases to Mr Charteris, a retired solicitor, who waited for her outside on the pavement. Enjoying a moment's peace he stood chatting to like-minded husbands whilst puffing contentedly on his curly pipe. Shopping done, they made their way across the high street to the coffee shop. Mrs Charteris came in first and sat at a table for two, whilst her husband went to the counter to place their order. They smiled politely across the room at acquaintances but as usual chose to sit alone. Judith found herself wondering if all aspects of their relationship was carried out with such precision, and smiled quietly to herself for having such a wicked thought.

Then there was Mrs Lloyd, a mother of four with several grand-children, who liked nothing better than befriending all who dared to sit with her. She spent at least an hour in the cafe every day, and would beckon customers to join her as they came in. She loved to hear all the latest gossip and because people felt comfortable with Mrs Lloyd they off-loaded their troubles with ease. Some people thought she was just plain nosy but, to her credit, she was a dependable soul who never failed to come to the rescue in their hour of need.

Old Mr Jarvis came into the cafe at twelve sharp every Friday morning. He would park his motorised scooter against the wall and hobble slowly inside. Shuffling in on two sticks he carried his groceries in a dirty old linen shopping bag that had long since seen better days. Fiercely independent, he lived alone but ate his lunch at various establishments in the village each weekday. Friday was cafe day and as he sat down the waitress confirmed with him that he would eat his usual all day breakfast. A pleasant man by all accounts, but because of poor hygiene that was obnoxiously clear, the owners requested he sat alone in the corner, a safe distance from other cafe users.

"Do you mind if I share your table?" a man's voice asked Judith as she idly contemplated what breed of dog she would consider to keep her company in her dotage.

"No, not at all," she replied, and glanced up to see a middle-aged man taking the seat opposite her. Judith moved her tray across the table and found herself momentarily drawn to the dark-haired stranger. "Nice morning. Are you just visiting?" she enquired, attempting to make polite conversation without sounding over-friendly. Whoever this man was, she found herself strangely attracted to him and for a split second all thoughts of a four-legged friend went out the cafe door!

"Well, yes and no. To be honest, I've inherited Birch House down the road from here. My uncle passed away some time back and being the only surviving relative, he left the property to me. I'm used to city life really, so it has been a big decision to leave all that behind. I move here permanently in two weeks." As he stirred his coffee he gave her a warm smile. "How about yourself, have you lived here long?"

"I've been here about a year, so I'm just about settled now. I live in the lane just up from the beach. Like you, I was a townie before I came here so it's been a bit of a culture shock, but it's a lovely area and I don't regret the move."

They finished their coffee in an awkward silence but as they got up to leave the cafe together Judith spontaneously said, "If you want a break from unpacking I'm always here at this time on a Friday. We could have coffee together."

"That will be great," he smiled. "I look forward to seeing you again very soon."

Reaching for the door Judith looked at Mrs Lloyd who gave them both a reassuring smile as much as to say, your friend was right and perhaps pigs do fly after all!

JC

THE HAUNTING OF
MEREDITH BROWN

It took me a long time to get over the death of my father.
Probably because he was such a strong, rather combustible
personality, there was such a void without him. It wasn't as
if we were very close. In fact our relationship was a constant
battle of wills, usually me struggling to persuade him to my
point of view and him stubbornly refusing to see it.

'Dad,' I'd said through gritted teeth, 'you just
don't understand. '

'No, and I don't want to,' he'd said emphatically. 'People
didn't live together in my day. Your mum and I - well, she
went to the altar...you know...pure... '

He was too embarrassed to use the word 'virgin'. He was
too insensitive to realise that mum had been his slave,
willingly fading away as she'd pandered to his every whim.
Mum had become more of a shadow towards the end, her
personality completely washed out by his dominating
presence. But that's what made her happy, that's what
many of her generation had believed in. And he wouldn't
accept that Mike and I wanted to become a couple on an
equal partnership, that we wanted to buy a house in both
our names, that neither of us wanted to be 'the boss.'

'It's no good trying to make you see what I mean... '

'No, it isn't. Your mum and I. ... ' Funny how he also
referred to her first as if she'd made all the decisions.

That was the last battle I had with him. We were busy
moving ourselves in to our new house a couple of weeks
later, when my mobile rang.

'Is that Meredith Brown?' I didn't recognise the voice.
'This is Glenford Hospital. Could you possibly come in as
soon as possible? It's concerning Mr. Brown, your father.

He was brought in earlier.'

Of course we were too late. That choleric temperament had – literally – been the death of him. An angry rant at next-door's cat as it dug in his pristine rose bed had sent a surge to his heart that clutched and choked and stopped it beating. The neighbour, hiding behind her long curtains from his wrath, had watched him, but as soon as she'd seen him fall, had rushed to his help. Unlike a television hospital programme, there was no miraculous recovery so by the time we reached Accident and Emergency, he was quietly lying in a side room, waiting for us.

'So sorry,' said the harassed Sister on duty. 'The paramedics did all they could but... '

The next few weeks passed in an exhausting blur. We hadn't even completed the move, there was all that official procedure concerning a sudden death, the funeral to arrange, then we had dad's house to sort out. And the grief.

Three months later, we were still sifting through stuff in the sitting-room bureau, convinced that we would never reach the end of clearing out. We hadn't bothered to draw the curtains and a full moon peered at us from behind racing clouds. Every now and then the wind would lift and rattle the door knocker as it had all through my childhood here; I was used to the noise.

'Look at these photos, Mike.' I handed him an album I hadn't know existed. They were pictures of mum and dad on holiday in a Butlin's Camp, both coyly posing in hilarious nineteen fifties bathing costumes and grinning inanely. Each print had a hand-written caption of explanation.

'Was this their chalet?'

I realised what he'd said. '**Their** chalet?' I gasped. 'Do you mean they shared one?' Quickly, I grabbed the album back and read the incriminating words below; *The love nest we shared.* 'The old hypocrite!' As I seethed at his duplicity, there was an almighty crash upstairs.

'What on earth was that?' Mike leapt to his feet and hurried to investigate. The room suddenly felt very cold. I felt as if an icy finger was slowly stroking the back of my neck. Hastily I shoved the album back in the drawer.

'Mike!' I shouted. There was no answer. Clutching my cardigan around me, I stumbled up the stairs. 'Mike! What's happened?'

'In here.' A muffled voice came from what had been the spare bedroom. The shadeless bulb swung erratically casting eerie shadows on the walls. A figure writhed by the window, swathed in the red velvet curtain that had come crashing off the wall complete with heavy wooden pole.

'Damn thing just fell off,' grumbled Mike as he struggled to unwrap the crimson shroud. Through the window I could see the anguished face on the moon, blue with cold. The primeval wail of a tom-cat sizing up an opponent sent its strangled tones lurching across the night.

'Shall we pack up now?' I shivered. 'Finish tomorrow?'

But tomorrow brought more surprises. We were both tired after a long day at work- me at a nursery and Mike at a Manchester meeting and reluctant to look in the bureau again. So were sorting through some books on the dining-room table, when the 'phone in the hall began to ring. Automatically going to answer it, I froze in the doorway.

'Mike! It's not connected.'

'Must be a B.T. quirk.' He was very nonchalant but I could tell he was puzzled. 'Hello,' I heard him say cautiously. There was a silence, then, 'I'll tell her.'

'Wha...who was it?' My hands were trembling. I clutched at the table.

He looked at me. 'You'll not believe this ... It was a tele-engineer. They can connect electronically if they want to. Asked to speak to a Miss Brown. Said he'd had complaints yesterday from some old fellow at this number that a woman kept trying to break into his conversation and to tell Miss Brown that.'

'His conversation? From a dead 'phone?'

'Just explaining what he said.' Mike sounded tetchy. The last emotional months were beginning to affect us badly. I found myself becoming equally irritated by Mike - why couldn't he be strong, forceful. ...more like dad? Why did he always do what I asked?

'Right,' he said emphatically, almost as if he'd read my mind. 'We're going home. And we're locking this place up for a couple of weeks. Think we need to get away somewhere this weekend.'

My spirits lifted. As I went to close the front door, a tremendous gust of wind snatched it from my hands and slammed it shut, making the letterbox reverberate like maniacal laughter.

It was three weeks before we felt refreshed enough to go back to the house. As we drew up outside, the cat-owning-neighbour appeared in her well-lit front door.

'Meredith, my dear,' she began, 'I don't want to worry you but - 'I had a horrible feeling that I was about to be worried '- there have been some peculiar noises coming from next-door. Lots of banging, doors slamming and I'm sure I heard music.'

My heart sank further. It was almost as if we'd never been away.

'Thanks, Mrs Jacobs,' and I hurried up our path as she craned inquisitively over the dividing fence.

The hall was littered with mail. A large pink envelope was

prominent amongst the letters. The handwriting was so familiar I almost dropped it as I felt a wave of sickness sweep through me. Then I looked at the date stamp; the day and month, thirteenth February, was only last week....but the year was 1993. Dad's handwriting. The month and year my mum died. The envelope was still sealed. I could hardly breathe.

Mike was standing close behind me.

'What's the matter?'

Shaking my head, I looked in the sitting-room. The bureau had been emptied on to the floor, papers, letters, documents scattered in a frenzy as if someone had been searching for something. The old Dansette record player was open and a black disc on the turntable. I looked at the title - Pat Boone, *Love Letters in the Sand.* Circa 1957!

Even more chaos in the dining room - the books thrown around, some open, some on the floor, again as if there had been a frantic search going on.

Taking the card with me, I went into the kitchen. Two mugs – clean – were side by side on the table. Carefully I sat down.

'Do you think - ' I began, but Mike interrupted me. 'Now don't start getting fanciful. I noticed a window in the dining-room on the latch. Someone's obviously broken in and been looking for valuables. Probably just going to make a drink when they were interrupted.'

I nodded, too dazed to argue. And that's what I wanted to believe. Not that Dad was still restlessly present here, too unhappy or bewildered to be at peace. What was he – they – looking for?

'Drink this.' Mike was becoming more positive. I liked it, it reminded me of someone. 'Just going to look upstairs. You okay?'

I nodded, then as soon as he'd gone, crept back to the sittingroom. Scrabbling through the papers strewn over the floor, I knew exactly what was missing – the photo album. No-one would steal that. And the window had been tightly shut. Mike was trying to rationalise everything.

'Now,' he said firmly - I hadn't heard him come into the room – 'I've decided. We're going to get professional house clearers in. Can't bear to see you getting so upset. You've got just this evening to take anything you want to keep, then the rest goes. '

'What was upstairs?'

'Nothing. Just more chaos.' I didn't want to find out.

There wasn't much in the end. I took a couple of books that had been dad's favourites, their wedding picture in the silver frame, *Love Letters* and *Magic Moments*. Everything else miraculously disappeared; cleared, the house was calm and sold quickly.

Later that year, on a summer's evening, I was reading quietly while listening to the radio, when *Love Letters* came over the air. Just as it finished the doorbell began to chime. No-one was there when Mike opened the door. And then I realised – we didn't have a doorbell....

JS

A TIER FOR JANE

I am a ghost, it is my job. Well it is now, ever since my tragic demise in a motorway accident three months ago. One minute I was cruising the fast lane and the next a lorry crossed the central reservation and BANG!

I left behind my wife, Jane, and my three-year-old son Danny. Ever since my death, I have been here in what is called the Second Tier. It is not a bad place, sort of a fluffy Earth really. I don't really feel any hunger or discomfort. There are classes to attend and the other entities are very kind.

Everyone who dies comes to Second Tier to have their life evaluated. Those good people will move on to First Tier and those who have been particularly bad will go straight to Third Tier. The main difference is that if you work very hard in the Third Tier, over many lifetimes you can find yourself back in Second Tier. You may then get an opportunity to rise to the First Tier. This is what I am aiming for. I didn't live too holy a life on Earth, so I suppose the Third Tier is what I can expect.

I just know that Jane will go directly to the First Tier because she is such a good person and I want to be able to see and hold her again. That's the only pain I feel now, the pain of loss and separation from my family. I am told that this will gradually subside. I have also been encouraged to visit my loved ones and re-assure them that I am well. Once we move on to another tier, movement to Earth is impossible.

I learnt that you have to visit a special place, and you have to meditate very hard and transport yourself to your loved one. A leader will fetch me when it is time to go. I cannot wait.

The Second Tier is a crowded place; there are thousands of languages being spoken but somehow I hear them all in English. There was a very useful class I attended today on materialisation, which was given by a Chinese tutor. Materialisation seems to be very much like moving to Earth. You meditate very deeply and your vision should appear made up mostly of plasma. The better you are at it, the clearer your image will be.

It seemed a very long time before a Leader arrived to take me to the meditation area. The area was made up of a sort of rocky outcrop and the rocks were covered in a soft green moss. There was a warm light shining down on to the rocks, which I didn't recognise as sunlight but was just as warming. As I sat down, I automatically turned my face into the light and felt its warm glow enter my body through my closed eyes. The leader told me just to relax.

"It may take some time for you," he said.

I closed my eyes and tried to picture Jane and Danny as clearly as possible. After what seemed an age I slowly opened my eyes. I was still seated on the rocks.

"Just relax and imagine being with them and what you will feel," the Leader said. I closed my eyes again. I imagined Jane lying in bed alone, Danny lying in his little bed. This time tears ran down my face and I felt myself crying out aloud.

When I opened my eyes, the light had gone. I was confused for a moment and then realised I was in a darkened room. It was my bedroom – I couldn't believe it. I moved towards the bed and I saw Jane lying on her side facing me. I rushed to her wanting to pick her up in my arms but then realised I didn't have any. I knew that I would be invisible unless I materialized and even then, I would only be a plasma version of me. This was not going

to be easy.

I sat down on the bed beside her, willing her to wake up. As I sat down, Jane sat up and looked around blindly in the dark. This was fantastic; I must have some presence after all.

"Come on Jane, it's me," I said.

She immediately pulled the duvet up to her chin.

"Go away," she screamed.

I stood up again.

"It's alright Jane; I just want to tell you that I'm ok. Don't be afraid, please."

Jane by now had pulled the duvet right over her head and was hiding beneath it.

"No, no," she sobbed.

I did not know what to do. Then I thought I could materialize. If she could see me, she would be fine. I closed my eyes and concentrated, but my mind was still racing.

After a few minutes, I opened my eyes and saw that the room was lit by a blue green glow. I went to the mirror and all I saw was a wispy glow of light, which appeared to be coming from my arm area. Jane was still sobbing and all I could think of was not upsetting her any more.

I went into Danny's room and wished I could kiss him. He looked so peaceful despite Jane's crying and sobbing. I closed my eyes again and concentrated on returning. When I opened my eyes I was back on the sunny rocks. I felt utterly dejected and exhausted.

The leader took hold of me.

"These things can be quite hard at first."

"I've ruined everything. She was terrified," I said.

"It's always difficult when you try to contact a loved one. Humans spend so much of their time frightening each other about the afterlife that they are bound to be scared when confronted by an apparition."

"I can't go back, she was so frightened."

"Well I believe you should. None of you know how long you will remain on this tier and it may be your only chance to make contact."

"I'm scared, I don't want to frighten her again," I said.

"We will leave it for a couple of Earth days and try again. You have experience now. You should make sure you can control your voice – what seems normal to you can come out booming if you are excited. Try to reassure her, think of some circumstance that means a lot to both of you. Convince her that it is really you behind the voice." I thanked the Leader and returned to my normal station feeling very bruised.

I thought very hard over the next time period. Perhaps I had gone in there without thinking it through. I must admit I did panic, maybe my voice was booming out. I thought about it and turned it over and over in my mind. I had to give it another go. I would think of something personal to tell her and she would realise she was safe.

The Leader eventually led me to the meditation place where I took up position. I closed my eyes and faced into the warm light. I kept telling myself to keep calm and just concentrate deeply on my family. The pictures I created seemed so vivid that I could almost touch them and almost immediately the light seemed to go out. I opened my eyes and saw Jane sitting up in bed reading. She looked stunning and although I had no discernable body my heart leapt. Once again, I wanted to rush over to her and hug her but I told myself I couldn't mess up this time.

"Jane, darling," I whispered.

She looked up startled.

"Jane, it's alright, I'm here because I love you both. You're not going mad."

She was looking around wildly, the book fell to the floor and for a moment I thought she was about to run away.

"It's me – David. You know, the football mad one. The one who proposed to you in the car park of Fulham United."

She looked in the direction of the sound. Her mouth moved slowly and she said, "David, you're frightening me – what do you want?"

I was excited but kept my voice low.

"We are allowed to come back to a loved one and tell them that we are safe. I tried before but I messed it up. I don't have long down here, you must believe me when I say I am fine and being well looked after. One day we will be together again I am sure of it."

She began to cry.

"David, I have missed you so much. Danny and I will

never forget you."

"Will you come with me to see Danny?" I said.

"Of course," she choked.

She walked into Danny's room.

"I wish we could see you David, just once more."

"I'm afraid I am a bit of a failure at materialization, but maybe I will get another chance. Can you kiss him for me?"

She bent forward and kissed Danny's forehead. She stood up wiping tears from her face.

"I have to go darling. If I can I will come back, if not have a happy life and live it to the full," I said.

She blew a kiss and I closed my eyes. When I opened them again the bright light was shining on me. The Leader approached.

"I can see by your face that you have connected successfully. You will find things much easier from now on," he said.

I don't know how long I have left on the Second Tier but I do know I will get to the First Tier if it takes me five lifetimes. I know Jane will be waiting there one day.

BH

EVENING

Day's end
Calm and still.
The storm has passed.
Chill shadows
creep over the lawn.
Ink-spatters of birds
swoop high
through the cloud-scattered sky.
A canvas of scarlet light
slides slowly away,
drawing velvet darkness
over the fading day.
It ends.
Calm and still.

JS

LIST OF SPONSORS
IN ORDER OF RECEIPT

T & M Engineering, Metheringham
Moy Park, Anwick
Mr. Wilder, Ruskington
R.C. Setchfield, Grantham
Mrs Webber, Grantham
Mr & Mrs Holden, Grantham
Mark Brown, Grantham
Mrs B. Fearn, Grantham
Retail Eyes, Milton Keynes
Antonio de Souza, Scoffers, Sleaford
Maurkare Cleaning, Sleaford
Co-operative Society, Lincolnshire
Anonymous donor
RAF Waddington [Sponsoring poems]
RAF Cranwell
The Lions Club, Sleaford
The Buffaloes, Sleaford
Martin Bland Motorcycles, Sleaford
Mr. P Rigby, Grantham
Anon
M. Mountain, Sleaford
Donations of stationery - anon.
Q.K. Coldstore, Marston
Blue Cube, Milton Keynes
The Queens Head, Kirkby-la-Thorpe
Solo Club, Sleaford
Patrick Ooi, Cream Magazines, St. Ives, Cambs.

We are indebted to these warm-hearted sponsors without whom it would have been impossible to produce the Anthology. It is especially gratifying as times are bleak at the moment - and these generous donations have contributed to a money-raising event for the St Andrew's Children's Hospice in Grimsby, Lincolnshire.

Thank you.

ABOUT THE HOSPICE.

St. Andrew's Children's Hospice opened in March 2001 and serves the area of Lincolnshire and East Yorkshire caring for children and young people aged from birth to 22 years who have a progressive life-limiting condition.

Caring for a seriously ill child, often twenty-four hours a day, seven days a week over many years, places a huge emotional and physical strain on the whole family. The Hospice helps by welcoming them into a purpose-built, friendly and homely environment where staff can offer both physical care and emotional support.

All care is provided completely free of charge. However, less than 5% of their income is from statutory funding and the Hospice is largely dependant on public donations.

All the money raised from this book will go directly to St. Andrew's Children's Hospice.

If you would like to know more about St. Andrew's Hospice telephone 01472 3550908 or visit their website at standrewshospice@nelpct.nhs.uk.

JC